Seven Days in Sydney

Photographed from the Ritz Cremorne

For Roger
and
Margaret

Published by
DAVID MESSENT PHOTOGRAPHY
SYDNEY AUSTRALIA
First Edition Published 1988
Revised and updated 1989
Revised and updated 1991
Revised and updated 1992
Revised and updated 1993
Reprinted 1994
Revised and updated 1996
Revised and updated 1998

Copyright
National Library of Australia
ISBN No. 0 646 33966 4

Text   : David Messent & Graham White
Design   : Ian Richards
Photography   : David Messent
Helicopters   : Heli-Aust, Helicopter Charter
                and Sydney Helicopter Service
Maps   : Gregory's Publishing, a division
                of Universal Press Pty Ltd.
Typesetting   : Max Peatman
Assembly   : Max Peatman

Colour Separations: Sinnott Bros. Sydney.
Printed in Singapore by Kyodo.

Contents

Introduction

Sydney was born in seventeen eighty eight. Just a baby compared with Rome, Athens, Tokyo, Moscow or any other major city you care to mention. Yet what our city has to offer eclipses any other traditional tourist destination in the world. True, we may not have a Colisseum or a Parthenon, but we do have a fascinating colonial history. This history is not bound up in mystery and legend, but is right there to be examined for the asking; the journals of First Fleet sailors and the despatches of the first Governors can be viewed on micro-film at the Mitchell Library and the State Archives, while houses, stores, churches and public buildings dating from the first decades of the colony still exist in Sydney.

Anyway, who needs a Parthenon when we've got the Opera House. Surrounded on three sides by sparkling blue water, its white sails glistening in the sunshine, the Opera House stands on its own as an example of modern architecture. Try to think of another modern building to compare with it. Then there's the Harbour Bridge; still the widest steel arch bridge in the world; it identifies Sydney as surely as the name on an atlas. But the bridge and Opera House would be nothing without Sydney Harbour, Sydney's raison d'être. 'To see Sydney Harbour' is the reason most tourists give for visiting Sydney.

Forget muggings in New York and civil strife elsewhere, Sydney is a safe place to visit. Forget snow in Montreal and drizzle in London, Sydney's climate is pleasant throughout the year. Summers are warm to hot, winters are mild, spring and autumn are perfect, while rainfall comes in short sharp bursts so most days are sunny. Forget Cannes, Malibu, Rio and Waikiki, Sydney's beaches, in particular the 13 beaches on the Pacific Ocean between Manly and Palm Beach, are the best in the world. And forget Paris cuisine. Sydney's restaurants are excellent and cater for every conceivable taste at locations from Rasputin's Russian Restaurant to the Woolloomooloo Woolshed.

When it comes down to it you don't go to see a city to lie on the beach or sit in a restaurant, but to see the sights, which I hope this book will help you to do. Most tourists visit Sydney for a week or less, so I've covered the most interesting places to visit if you only have seven days to spare. All the tours start and finish at Circular Quay, which is served well by ferries, trains, buses and taxis and is within walking distance of most of Sydney's major hotels. The maps at the back of the book cover Darling Harbour and Sydney town centre in detail, and the rest of the metropolitan area as a route map. To follow the tours that go out of the city, the purchase of a Gregory's Street Directory of Sydney is recommended, in particular for the tours of Wednesday and Thursday, which are easier if you have a car. So start each day at the map of Circular Quay on page 170, and enjoy your stay in Sydney!

David Messent

MONDAY

Monday

Harbour scenery and Australian wildlife

Walk through The Rocks and up Bridge Stairs to the Harbour Bridge, then climb to the top of the Pylon Lookout for a magnificent view of Sydney Harbour. After crossing the bridge, a cab ride takes you via North Sydney to an old gun battery at Bradleys Head. Following a short harbourside walk and a visit to the zoo, return to Circular Quay by ferry.

I guess there couldn't be a more logical point to start a tour of Sydney than with the *Harbour Bridge*. Dominating Sydney's skyline since it was completed in 1932, the Bridge has become an unofficial symbol of Sydney to people all around the world, while its pedestrian footpath and south-east pylon provide a vantage point for spectacular views of the city, *Opera House* and harbour.

Museum of Contemporary Art

Follow the pavement on the west side of *Circular Quay* through *First Fleet Park* to George Street. Turn right on George Street and the first building you reach is the *Museum of Contemporary Art*. This squat sandstone structure was once the Maritime Services Board building, and maritime motifs decorate the exterior high above the entrance way. The museum is custodian to one of Australia's major collections of modern art, representing the work of over 500 artists from around the world including Henry Moore and Picasso. Included among the works on display are paintings by Dr John Wardell Power whose bequest to Australia for the pursuit of the "plastic arts" led to the founding of the museum. New exhibitions are frequently displayed in the galleries, often of a rather puzzling nature!

Circular Quay and the Sydney skyline (below) a far cry from the scene that greeted Governor Phillip when he arrived with the First Fleet in 1788. Phillip chose Sydney Cove from the multitude of bays in the Harbour as the "one which had the finest spring of water, and in which ships can anchor… close to the shore." He named the new settlement 'Sydney' after Thomas Townshend, First Viscount Sydney, British Home Secretary 1784-89, who had ordered the sending of the fleet. In this picture the liner QE2 is moored at Sydney Cove Passenger Terminal, as the Manly ferry "Queenscliff" departs from Circular Quay.

(Previous pages) The liner "Asuka" approaching Circular Quay

George Street, the oldest street in Australia, (left), was first called Spring Row because it followed the line of the track that led to the freshwater "spring" of the Tank Stream near the present site of Martin Place. It was named High Street by Governor King, and finally George Street in 1810 by Governor Macquarie after the "Mad Monarch" George III.

Buildings on the west side of George Street (left) stand on the site of the first hospital in Sydney, built by 12 convict carpenters and 16 crew from First Fleet transports. Though by November 1788 Governor Phillip wrote that the hospital was still 'not half finished, nor fit to receive an object.' The Fortune of War Hotel in the centre of the picture, dating to the 1920s, has held a liquor licence since 1839.

The Museum of Contemporary Art, (bottom left) occupies a building that used to be the headquarters of the Maritime Services Board. The Maritime Services Board building, in its turn, was built on the site of the four storey "Commissariat Stores", one of Sydney's oldest convict-built structures, opened by Macquarie in 1812, which was demolished without ceremony in 1940.

The noble span of Sydney Harbour Bridge (top right). The top of the arch of the bridge is 134 metres (440 feet) above the harbour. It was the tallest structure in Sydney from 1932 until the completion of Australia Square Tower in 1967. The top of the arch rises by up to 18 centimetres due to thermal expansion on hot summer days. When the bridge was opened the toll was 6d per passenger in a car, 3d for motorcycles or for a horse and rider, 2d per head of cattle and 1d per head of sheep or pigs. The Harbour Bridge is not the longest steel arch bridge in the world, but it is listed in the Guinness Book of Records as the widest, with a deck 49 metres wide.

(Following pages) The Manly jetcat 'Sea Eagle' passing Sydney Opera House as a thunderstorm blows in from the south. Photographed from the pedestrian walkway of the Harbour Bridge.

Circular Quay West (below) with P & O's Island Princess moored at Sydney Cove Passenger Terminal.

Monday

The Russian liner 'Southern Cross' (above) approaching Sydney Cove. Photographed from the pedestrian walkway of the Harbour Bridge.

The liner 'Crystal Harmony' at Sydney Cove Passenger Terminal. Vessels have moored at the location ever since January 1788 when ships of the First Fleet dropped anchor in the cove.

Right page : The colonial style North Sydney Post Office and Courthouse (top right) was once the tallest building in North Sydney and could be seen for miles in all directions. Now it's hemmed in by skyscrapers.

St Peter's Church and Vicarage on Blues Point Road at North Sydney (bottom right).

Turn right on George Street outside the museum then left on Argyle Street. Stay on the north pavement of Argyle Street for 200 metres, and ascend *Argyle Steps* to your right near a concrete bridge over the road. At the top of the steps turn left on the path in Cumberland Street and cross over to Bridge Stairs that lead up to the pedestrian footway of the Harbour Bridge.

Sydney Harbour Bridge

The opening ceremony for the Harbour Bridge took place on the roadway just south of the Harbour Bridge pylons on March 19, 1932. The ceremony was turned into a fiasco when Francis de Groot, an Irish member of the New Guard, slashed through the opening ribbon with his sword before the Premier could cut it with scissors, crying he was declaring the bridge open 'on behalf of decent and loyal citizens of New South Wales'. The New Guard was a private anti-communist organisation, which was affronted by the idea of the Labour Premier of New South Wales, Jack Lang, opening the bridge instead of a member of the Royal family or the King's representative, the Governor of New South Wales. A member of the New Guard, Captain de Groot, donned his old Hussar regiment uniform and followed the Governor's escort on horseback onto the Bridge. Nobody took any notice of de Groot on the Bridge and he waited patiently through the opening speeches for his cue, when he spurred his horse forward and cut through the ribbon, with his sword when it was stretched across the road.

De Groot was bundled off his horse, arrested and charged, and at his trial found guilty of offensive behaviour in a public place and of injuring government property... 'to wit one ribbon', and fined five pounds with four pounds costs. In his last known statement about the affair before he died in 1969 in a Dublin nursing home, de Groot said, 'I had opened the Harbour Bridge and that was all that mattered'.

Monday

From the footway you can look down on *The Rocks* area of Sydney, the first part of Australia settled by Europeans when the First Fleet arrived in 1788; or at least what is left of it; 300 buildings were demolished in The Rocks when the Harbour Bridge and approaches were built. On the bridge itself a constant stream of traffic passes by. During the rush hour 15,000 vehicles sometimes cross the Bridge every hour, over double the estimated maximum capacity of 6,000 an hour calculated when the Bridge was designed. The two traffic lanes next to the walkway carried trams until 1958, when the lines were pulled up and the new road lanes opened in July 1959.

The Pylon Lookout

The footway soon leads you to the south-east example of one of the 'Pillars of Hercules bestriding the tide', as The Sydney Morning Herald in 1932, dubbed the pairs of pylons gracing both ends of the Bridge. The hollow 89 metre high pylons, constructed from 18,000 cubic metres of granite quarried at Moruya on the south coast of New South Wales, are aesthetic and serve no particular structural purpose. A steel staircase through the inside of the pylon leads up to a display area with photos of the construction of the Bridge and examples of the rivets and steel used in fabrication. An open air observation lookout is right at the top. The pylon is usually open from 10.00am to 5.00pm, and there is a small entrance charge.

Harbour Views

Walk across the Harbour Bridge, through the north west pylon and down the steps near *Milsons Point* railway station to Broughton Street. Head down Broughton Street through the park and relax for a while on one of the benches facing the water to enjoy the spectacular

view; the panorama of the Opera House, city, Sydney Harbour and the Harbour Bridge.

If you are feeling a little more energetic, walk up Kirribilli Road, turn right into Waruda Avenue, then right again into Waruda Street where you will find *Mary Booth Reserve*. The reserve was named after Dr Mary Booth, a militant feminist, born in 1868, who believed that "good wives make good husbands"!

Bradfield Park, at the north end of the Harbour Bridge, is named after Dr J.J.C. Bradfield, appointed in 1912 to formulate a proposal for construction of a harbour crossing.

Under the park runs *Sydney's Harbour Tunnel*, opened in 1992. The idea of a second harbour crossing was first mooted in the 1950s, and a number of different schemes were announced, then shelved, before construction of the present tunnel was started in 1988. Tunnels through sandstone descend beneath the shoreline on each side of the harbour, and the space between is linked by hollow concrete sections, which were cast at Botany Bay, floated into position, then sunk into a trench of the harbour bed and joined together. The tunnel, costing $750 million, was completed by a joint venture company incorporating Australia's 'Transfield' and Japan's 'Kumagai Gumi'.

North Sydney

Follow Olympic Drive through Bradfield Park beneath the soaring span of the Harbour Bridge and hail a cab on Alfred Street. Turn left into Lavender Street, then right into Blues Point Road. A short distance along Blues Point Road on the left is the neat little sandstone church and vicarage of St. Peters. Follow Blues Point Road into Miller Street. At the junction of Mount Street and the Pacific Highway at Victoria Cross stands the Victorian colonial style

Aerial view of North Sydney (below).

Aerial view of Sydney City and Harbour with Bradleys Head in the foreground (right). The mast of H.M.A.S. Sydney can be picked out on the left of the headland.

19

When the gun batteries at Bradleys Head (top) were completed in 1871, they had a clear line of fire to the Harbour. Now the view is obscured by trees. The Russian Pacific Fleet was considered the biggest threat at the time.

'Victoria Regina' 1871 (above), neatly inscribed in the stonework.

Neat stone trenches (right) connect the gun emplacements.

The main entrance to Taronga Zoo (top).

The harbourside track at Bradleys Head (left).

The cuddly koala (above). This one is at the Koala Park at West Pennant Hills in Sydney, where you can get closer to the animals than at the Zoo.

Summer storm clouds over the city (top) photographed from Bradleys Head.

The elephant enclosure at Taronga Zoo (above).

North Sydney Post Office and Court House. The building is in the same mould as similar colonial buildings found in outposts of the former British Empire from Barbados to Khartoum to Delhi. On the south corner of the Pacific Highway and Mount Street, occupying an old bank building is a McDonald's restaurant. A plaque inside proudly announces that it is the 9,000th McDonalds opened in the world.

Continue on Miller Street, turn right on Berry Street and follow the one-way system along Arthur Street to the bridge over the Warringah Freeway near the tunnel toll booths for the Harbour Tunnel. Keep to the left after crossing the bridge and descend Kurraba Road to *Anderson Park.* The pioneer aviator Kingsford Smith once took off from Anderson Park in his bi-plane the *Lady Southern Cross.*

Neutral Bay at the end of the Park received its name in 1789, when Governor Phillip ordered that all foreign ships stopping in Sydney must anchor in 'Neutral Bay'. On the southern side of the bay, two or three submarines can usually be seen moored at HMAS *Platypus,* a submarine base commissioned in 1967 at the Australian Navy's torpedo repair and maintenance depot.

Bradleys Head

Follow the map through the back streets of Sydney's Lower North Shore suburbs past the Zoo into the virgin bushland of *Ashton Park,* then pay off the cab driver when the road reaches the old fortifications at *Bradleys Head.* Entry to the park is free during the week, but there is a small fee per car at weekends.

Three cannons mounted on carriages in gunpits at Bradleys Head are the best preserved example of a series of fortifications that were built on Sydney Harbour headlands during the 1870s.

Bradleys Head, named after Lieutenant William Bradley, a cartographer with the First Fleet who went on to become a Rear Admiral, was the first of Sydney's harbourside military reserves to be handed over for public recreation in 1908.

Descend the steps across the road from the cannons, which take you down to the harbour foreshore, where a ship's mast stands above the remains of some more old gunpits. The mast, from the cruiser *HMAS Sydney,* is a memorial to four men killed in action in the battle of the Cocos Islands on September 9, 1914. During the battle, the first in which a ship of the Royal Australian Navy took part, the Sydney sank the German raider 'Emden' and captured her crew. A stone pillar on the rocks just in front of the mast is one of the columns from the facade of the old Sydney G.P.O. building demolished in 1875. Between 1875 and 1912 ships ran speed trials between *Fort Denison,* a small fort that can be seen on an island in the direction of the Opera House and the pillar on Bradleys Head, which is exactly one nautical mile. The practice was stopped because of the danger to other vessels on the harbour.

Bush Walks

At the end of the car park on Bradleys Head, follow the path past the galvanised steel fence. Continue on the path for about a kilometre, through unspoilt bushland with views on the left across the harbour to the city. When the path reaches the road, follow it downhill for about 200 metres to the cable car, which takes you on a two-and-a-half minute ride over the hippos and alligators to the top entrance to *Taronga Zoo.*

Taronga Zoo

Taronga is aboriginal for 'beautiful view', and I believe that, without question, everyone would agree *Taronga Zoo,* on its location overlooking Sydney Harbour, is the most beautiful Zoo site in the world. Buy a copy of the Taronga Zoo guide and map at the shop near the entrance and search out some of Australia's unique wildlife. Koalas, kangaroos, emus, wombats, the duck-billed platypus and many examples of antipodean birds, reptiles and sea creatures, can all be found. There are also the everyday rhinos, big cats, apes and bears that help make up Taronga Zoo's total collection of approximately 3,000 marsupials, mammals, birds, reptiles and fish.

The Zoo is open from 9.00am to 5.00pm, although visitors can stay until sunset. As far as it can, the Zoo tries to be self-supporting, and you will notice the names of companies and individuals on many of the cages who sponsor the animals.

Exit by the lower entrance to the Zoo and walk down the hill to the wharf at the bottom of the road, from where a regular ferry service runs to Circular Quay. When Taronga Zoo opened in 1916, the animals, including Jessie the elephant, were shipped across the harbour from the old Moore Park Zoo by vehicular ferry and off loaded at the wharf.

Tonight, wander to The Rocks to enjoy a drink in one of the old pubs. If you are eating out, the Waterfront Restaurant or the Imperial Peking Harbourside, in Campbell's Storehouse, with a view across Circular Quay to the Opera House, would be hard to beat for atmosphere and a first-class meal.

TUESDAY

Colonial heritage and a trip by ferry

The first part of today's tour, a stroll up Macquarie Street, stopping at places of interest on the way, is a tribute to Governor Macquarie and his convict architect Francis Greenway. Then the rest of the day is taken up with a trip to Manly.

Governor Macquarie

Following the struggle to found the colony under Governor Phillip (1788-1792), fresh development was stifled in the first years of the 19th century through the influence of the New South Wales Corps or 'Rum Corps' as they were known, who were able to control the finances of Sydney by using Bengal Rum as a means of exchange, as there was a great scarcity of hard currency. An attempt to put the colony's affairs in order when Governor Bligh (of Mutiny on the Bounty fame) was sent out as Governor, ended in disaster in 1808 when the Rum Corps rose and deposed him. So when Brigadier General Lachlan Macquarie arrived in 1810 with his own regiment of Royal Highlanders, though he was able to break the control of the Rum Corps, the administration of Sydney was in a mess or as Macquarie put it:

"... I found the colony barely emerging from infantile imbecility and suffering from various privations and disabilities; the country impenetrable beyond 40 miles from Sydney; agriculture in a yet languishing state; commerce in its early dawn; revenue unknown; threatened by famine; distracted by faction; the public buildings in a state of dilapidation and mouldering to decay; the few roads and bridges formerly constructed, rendered almost impassable; the population depressed by poverty; no public credit nor private confidence; the morals of the great mass of the population in the lowest state of debasement and religious worship almost totally neglected.'.

During his 12 year term as Viceroy, ending in 1822, Macquarie certainly transformed Sydney from a state of 'infantile imbecility' into a more respectable colony. His achievements included the erection of over 200 public buildings and the granting of land for Sydney's two cathedrals, setting aside *Hyde Park* as a public park (1810) and founding the *Botanical Gardens* (1816), making the colony's first coinage (1813) and opening its first bank, the Bank of New South Wales (1817), promoting the first crossing of the *Blue Mountains* (1813) and founding the new settlements of Richmond, Windsor and Liverpool, on the plains around Sydney. Macquarie could upset people by his autocratic and arrogant style of leadership and his insufferable vanity – he named Macquarie Street after himself and Elizabeth Street after his wife, but there's no diminishing the work he did as Governor.

Macquarie hardly need have concerned himself about his name being carried forward for posterity; today in Sydney there are four Macquarie Avenues, three Macquarie Places, nine Macquarie Roads, seventeen Macquarie Streets, one Macquarie Drive, one Macquarie Grove, one Macquarie Terrace, one Macquarie University and one Macquarie Shopping Centre.

Justice and Police Museum

At the east end of Circular Quay head up Phillip Street and immediately left on Albert Street. On the corner of Albert and Phillip Streets, occupying an old sandstone Police Station and Courthouse is the *Justice and Police Museum*. On display is a fascinating array of weaponry taken from criminals over the years, including daggers, guns, hatchets, batons and maces, many used in evidence in murder trials and others used to commit murders which have remained unsolved. Included in the collection are revolvers and pistols captured from the bushrangers Ned Kelly, Ben Hall, Captain Moonlight and Thunderbolt Lightning. One haunting display includes 100 old black and white mug shots of criminals glaring from the walls and two death masks of criminals cast after they were hanged. A "Maxim for general guidance of members of the police force" published in 1870 included the instruction to '... display perfect command of temper under insult and provocation, to which all constables are occasionally liable'. And that 'every man (should) devote some portion of his spare time to the practice of reading and writing, and the general improvement of his mind, for ignorance is an unsuperable bar to promotion in the Police Service...'

*The western Royal Botanic Gardens and
Macquarie Street (below). Chifley Tower is
on the right side of the picture.*

Tuesday

At the end of Albert Street turn right on Macquarie Street past the entrance to the *Ritz Carlton Hotel.* The hotel, in a former Health Department building, has a foyer, bar and lounge resembling the interior of an English country mansion, with antique furniture, clocks, mirrors, ceramics and cut glass chandeliers.

The hotel is a far cry from the drab interior of the old Health Department, which housed the "Blue Light Clinic", a V.D. clinic that operated from the site from 1933 to 1986 when it was transferred to the Nightingale Wing of Sydney Hospital. In the 1940's patients files were marked "V.D." in bold letters with a special Health Department rubber stamp. The well-worn stamp is periodically on display with other mementoes that once belonged to the Health Department in a glass cabinet at Hyde Park Barracks.

Continue past a 1938 art deco style building to the *Inter-Continental Hotel* on the corner of Bridge and Macquarie Streets. If you've left without your breakfast go into the hotel cocktail lounge for a coffee. The lounge is in the courtyard of the former Treasury and Audit Office, designed by Colonial Architect Mortimer Lewis and built 1849-51. The first shipments from the Australian gold fields were stored in the Treasury strongroom.

Standing on the opposite corner of Bridge Street is the former *Colonial Secretary's Building* and the offices of the Minister for Works. Utzon stormed into the Public Works Minister's office on the first floor to tender his resignation as architect of the Sydney Opera House in February 1966. The Department of Public Works was housed in the building from 1875 until it moved to the State Office Block in 1967. A white marble statue of Victoria adorns the hall inside the main entrance to the Colonial Secretary's Building off Macquarie Street.

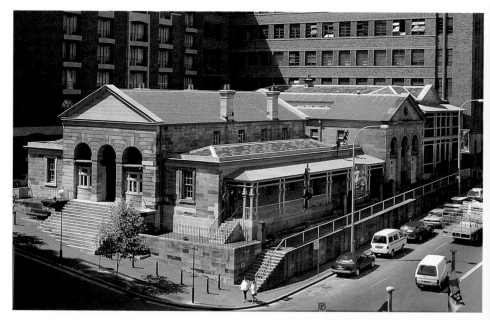

Left page : The Justice and Police Museum (top) occupies the old Water Police Station and Courthouse, in use from 1854 to 1984.

A sandstone relief on the east facade of the old Treasury building (centre).

Detail of decorative railing on the Treasury (bottom).

Lion capitals (left) decorate the stone balustrades of the Treasury.

The Treasury (below) is now part of the Inter-Continental Hotel.

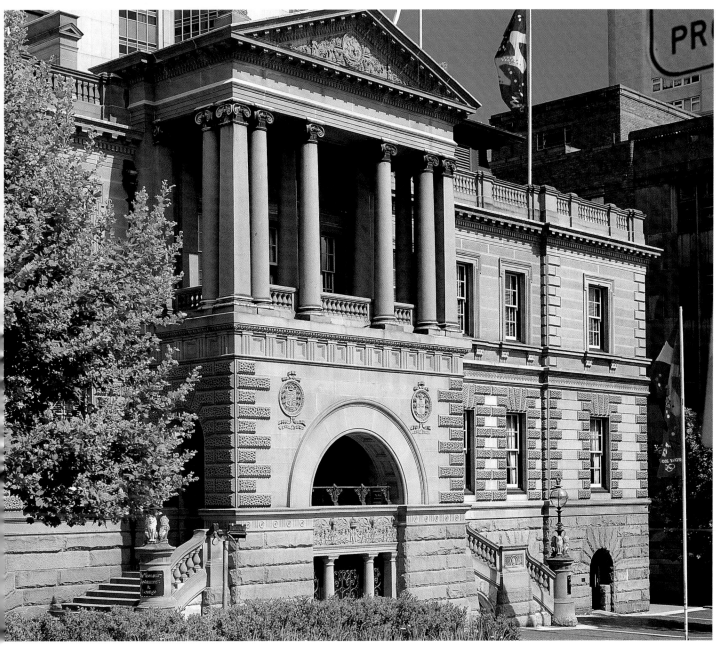

The Conservatorium of Music

Continue on Bridge Street past the statue of Edward VII on horseback to the castellated *Conservatorium of Music*. Free instrument recitals are given by students in the Conservatorium's Concert Hall during term time, check the times given on the noticeboard at the entrance. The Conservatorium was originally the stables for Government House.

Designed by Francis Greenway, an architect transported to Australia in 1814, for forging a signature on a building contract, who was appointed Civil Architect by Macquarie in 1816, the stables were intended for a palatial Government House that was never built. Commissioner J.T.Bigge, who arrived in Sydney in 1819 to conduct an enquiry into the affairs of the colony, stopped the building of Government House because the design was too costly and criticised Macquarie for making the stable 'such a palace for horses'. To passengers arriving in Sydney at the time, the stables were the biggest building on the horizon and they thought they were looking at Government House.

The Garden Palace

With the entrance to the Conservatorium of Music at your back, turn left, walk up the grass verge and go through the gate of the *Royal Botanic Gardens*, then turn right and follow the path. Where you are walking was the site of the *Garden Palace*, a splendid edifice built for an International Exhibition in 1879. The Palace, the biggest structure completed in Sydney up to that time, stretched from the Conservatorium of Music to the present site of the *State Library of New South Wales*. With a dome 64 metres high and a hall 244 metres long, it was longer and higher than the Queen Victoria Building in the city. The Palace burnt to the ground in 1882 only three years after it was completed. Sydney's first steam trams carried visitors to the Exhibition from Redfern Station to Macquarie Street in 1879.

As you are walking through the gardens glance to your right over the fence to the extraordinary art-deco style cream tiled facade of British Medical Association House (1929) at 135-137 Macquarie Street. Griffins support the overhanging bay windows, lions holding shields stand between the second floor windows, knights in armour squat on top of the buttresses while just below them, koalas clutch to the facade on either side of the building. The entrance hall and first floor landing of B.M.A. House, crafted from white stone, look like the entrance of a grand public baths.

One door down from B.M.A. House at 133 Macquarie Street is "History House", dating to 1871, containing the library and offices of the Royal Australian Historical Society. The public are welcome to use the Society's reference library on signing the visitor's book.

A little way up the street at 145 Macquarie Street is *The Royal Australian College of Physicians*. The college contains several examples of antique furniture donated by physicians over the years, and a collection of rare books on medicine, including hundreds of volumes over two hundred years old. Note the verandah columns of the two upper floors, which are a simpler Doric design to the Ionic columns of the ground and first floors. The lower two storeys date to 1849, the third storey was built later in the nineteenth century, and the fourth storey and attic were built in 1910.

Continuing on the path through the gardens you soon reach a fountain adorned with bronze statues by the Italian sculptor Simonetti, unveiled during Victoria's Diamond Jubilee Celebration in 1897. Standing tall on the central pedestal is Governor Phillip, clutching a flag in one hand and a proclamation in the other. A brick wall next to the path 50 metres south west of the fountain is a memorial to Captain Arthur Phillip. The wall is built of bricks from the seventeenth century house at Vernal's Farm, Lyndhurst in Hampshire, where Phillip lived before setting out on his voyage with the First Fleet. An oak tree a few metres away to the right of the wall was grown from an acorn from an ancient oak tree at Vernal's Farm.

Descend the steps in front of Phillip's memorial, pass through the Pioneers Garden and after three or four minutes walk reach the tropical glasshouses. The Arc Glasshouse contains exotic tropical plants, the Pyramid Glasshouse contains Australian tropical plants. There is a small entrance fee. Take the path back towards the city that runs west from the Arc Glasshouse and leave the gardens by the first exit you come to opposite the Public Library. Nearby on the corner of the park at the junction of Macquarie Street is a memorial to the horses of the Australian Desert Mounted Corps who fought in Palestine from 1915-18. "... They suffered wounds, thirst, hunger and weariness almost beyond endurance but never failed. They did not come home. We will never forget them." In one of the greatest feats in the history of mounted warfare, the horses carried the Corps to victory at Beersheba, charging an entrenched Turkish position to take the town with only light casualties. Cross the street to the Public Library of New South Wales.

The State Library

The *State Library*, Australia's oldest library founded in 1826, contains an excellent reference library and the Mitchell and Dixon collections, between them the greatest collection of Australiana in the world. *The Mitchell Library* contains such priceless items as Cook's diaries, the log from HMS *Bounty* and eight out of the ten existing journals written by members of the First Fleet (available for viewing on micro-film). Many of these treasures were donated in 1907 when David Scott

Mitchell gave his entire collection of 60,000 articles of Australiana to the state. Sir William Dixon, who started collecting when David Scott Mitchell finished, donated his own collection of 20,000 items of Australiana when he died in 1952. Covering most of the floor space in the lobby of the State Library is an intricately crafted representation of Abel Tasman's map of Australia in marble and brass.

The map is based on Tasman's voyage of discovery of 1642. Tasman only charted the south coast of Tasmania and interpolated Tasmania on his map as a landform joined to the continent of Australia. Look at the beautiful representations of explorers' ships acid etched into the glass of the lobby doors. A bold inscription on the east wall of the foyer announces "In books lies the soul of the whole past time, the articulate audible voice of the past when the body and material substance of it has altogether vanished like a dream". Check to see what exhibitions may be on in the galleries.

Leave the library by the main entrance, descend the stairs and turn left. Pass the statue of Matthew Flinders (1774-1814), a Captain in the Royal Navy, who explored and made the first reliable charts of a large portion of the Australian coast between 1796 and 1803. Flinders' use of the word "Australia" on his maps led to the acceptance of that name for the continent. On his return voyage to England he suffered the ignominy of being held captive by the French on Mauritius for six and a half years from 1803 to 1810 despite holding a French passport. Flinders used his time in captivity to complete many of his charts. Note the massive sandstone blocks used in the construction of *Wyoming* at 175 Macquarie Street across the road. The building, completed in 1911, was designed as professional medical chambers. In pleasant contrast to its heavy design is the Georgian style two storey *Horbury Terrace* (1842), next door at 173 Macquarie Street.

Continue south on Macquarie Street past the modern State Library building, opened in 1988. This is the *Macquarie Street Wing* of the State Library containing the General Reference Library. The licensed Glass House Cafe in the library is accessible from the main entrance off Macquarie Street.

Parliament House

The next building on the left is *New South Wales Parliament House*. The Georgian style double-storey verandahed building was built in 1811-1816 as the north wing to the *'Rum Hospital'* and converted for use by the State Legislative Council in 1829. It is the oldest Parliament in Australia. The 'Rum Hospital' received its name because in 1811 when Macquarie entrusted a triumvirate with the building of a new hospital, he paid them by granting them a monopoly on the import of rum into the Colony for three years.

Parliament House is open from 9.30am to 4.00pm on weekdays only. Members of the public are free to walk through the designated areas. Make sure you pick up an interesting little free booklet about Parliament House from the desk at the entrance.

Around the walls of the exhibition area towards the back of Parliament House, are two permanent photography displays, one in colour by David Moore on the Australian flora and landscape, and the other in black and white by Max Dupain of New South Wales' colonial period public works. In the Parliament House Library there is an illustrated history of the discovery and settlement of Sydney and the story of the New South Wales Parliament. Displayed in a glass case are the opal encrusted gold scissors that were officially, and I stress the word officially, used to open the Harbour Bridge in 1932. The same scissors were used to open the Glebe Island Bridge in 1995.

When Parliament is sitting, the action can be watched from the

public galleries of the Upper House *(Legislative Council)* and Lower House *(Legislative Assembly)*. When it is not sitting, which is most of the time, the public are free to go into the respective chambers. The shell of the Legislative Council Chamber is a pre-fabricated iron structure, that was originally sent to Australia from England to be used as a church in the goldfields. Due to a shortage of housing in Melbourne at the time, it was used for accommodation there before being bought by the New South Wales Government, dismantled and freighted to Sydney, then re-erected for the new Council Chamber.

Sydney Hospital

Sydney Hospital , next to Parliament House, occupies the ground where the central wing of the Rum Hospital once stood, demolished in 1880 to make way for the present structure. Behind the main building the *Florence Nightingale Wing*, opened in 1869 to receive nurses trained by Florence Nightingale, is the oldest part of the hospital.

Outside the hospital on Macquarie Street, the statue of Fiaschi the bronze wild boar was donated by a family in Florence whose relatives had worked as surgeons at the hospital. Patients rub its nose for good luck as they enter the hospital. As you walk pass, toss a dollar coin into the wishing fountain beneath the boar to help the hospital. An Italian flag flying from a pole next to the boar is donated by the Sydney Italian Consulate.

Macquarie had ordered the building of a new hospital in Sydney shortly after his arrival in the colony. The site, on a breezy elevated ridge east of the main town, was apparently the choice of Mrs Macquarie, who also made some sketch plans of the hospital buildings.

The deal Macquarie struck with the triumvirate charged with building the "Convict Hospital", stipulated "... the said contractors, shall be allowed and have permission to

The grand sandstone structure (top left) used to house the Colonial Secretary's office and the department of the Minister for Works. The Italian Renaissance style building was designed by Colonial Architect James Barnet and completed in 1876. Busts of English 19th century characters such as Charles Dickens, Benjamin Disraeli and William Gladstone, by Thomas Woolner (who also created the statue of James Cook in Hyde Park) decorate the Executive Council Chambers on the third floor.

The statue of Wisdom (top right) in the corner niche of the Colonial Secretary's Building gazing out towards Sydney Harbour and the Heads, is one of three statues by Giovanni Fontana on the south east corner of the building.

The marvellous facade of British Medical Association House on Macquarie Street (above left).

The entrance of the Secretary for Works (above) is on the west side of the Colonial Secretary's Building.

A statue of 'Labour' (above) is one of three occupying niches in the north west corner of the Colonial Secretary's Building. The others are 'Science' and 'Industry'.

The Conservatorium of Music (top right) was designed by convict architect Francis Greenway as a stables for Government House. Why build such a 'palace for horses' wrote Commissioner Bigge, sent to New South Wales in 1819 to report to the home government on the affairs of the Colony.

This statue of Edward VII on horseback (right) stands at the top of Bridge Street in front of the Conservatorium of Music.

Tuesday

Views of the western Royal Botanic Gardens with left page (top). The Pioneers Garden, (centre left) gateway to the gazebo in the rose garden, (centre right), 'The Huntsman', and (bottom) the Pyramid and Arc glasshouses.

Top left "Love led them" a statue in the centre of the Pioneers Garden, top right the statue and fountain of Governor Arthur Phillip, and (bottom) other figures decorating the fountain.

purchase or to import into the colony, the quantity of forty five thousand gallons of spirits… (and) while construction took place… His Excellency will grant no further permission for the importation of spirits… excepting only what Government may deem it necessary… for their own use and occasions…" In addition the contractors received 20 convict labourers, 20 draught bullocks and 80 oxen for slaughter. At this time the cost price of imported Bengali rum was 3 shillings a gallon which could be retailed in the colony at up to 50 shillings a gallon. This agreement was made despite the fact that Macquarie had received specific instructions from the home authorities to halt the use of rum as a medium of exchange. The leading partner in the triumvirate carrying out the building work was the acting principal surgeon, D'Arcy Wentworth, who had left England under a cloud after being charged with highway robbery. Wentworth had previously been suspended by Bligh for alleged misuse of public labour in hospitals, and had supported the insurrection against Bligh.

When the hospital was completed in 1816, it was two feet lower than marked on the plan and Macquarie insisted against the protestations of the contractors that they complete an equivalent amount of labour on other public buildings. The hospital had a high stone wall on the Macquarie Street frontage to prevent convict patients escaping. Patients, who included the city poor as well as convicts, were locked in the wards from evening to sunrise with no toilet facilities. Medicines handed out by convict nurses and wardsmen were often administered to the wrong patient. There was a great shortage of drugs, as orders of medicines

requisitioned from England could take up to three years to arrive and if a particular drug for a patient was not available, the next most suitable, in the opinion of the dispenser, was administered.

A mortuary had been overlooked in the design and one of the kitchens was converted into a "deadhouse". Blood letting was frequently employed, one particular patient suffering "brain fever" had 2lb. of blood removed in the morning and 3lb. in the evening, when he was allowed to get up and dropped dead. As no space was available for cooking, food was prepared by the patients themselves in the wards. There was no segregation of sexes – a measure thought completely unnecessary by the principal surgeon as it was well known all female patients were infected with venereal disease.

Surgeons from the hospital were required to attend flogging of prisoners at *Hyde Park Barracks* next door, because if the prisoner collapsed the punishment was stopped. Surgeon Imlay from the hospital was dismissed in 1831 after refusing to attend flogging duty. The hospital ceased treating convicts in 1848 when the last were removed to the Parramatta Factory.

Concerned at the woeful state of the hospital system, in 1866 Colonial Secretary, *Sir Henry Parkes* wrote to Florence Nightingale in England for advice. Florence Nightingale replied to Parkes' letter promising her full support, not only for the sake of advancing the cause of medicine but out of a sense of gratitude to the people of Australia for their contributions to the Nightingale Fund immediately following the Crimean War. Nightingale despatched Miss Osburn, with five nursing sisters under her charge trained in her new

nursing program, to establish and run Sydney's first training school for probationary nurses to be located at Sydney Hospital. It established a system of nursing that was to endure for a hundred years. The new "Nightingale Wing" was completed at Sydney Hospital for the use of the school in the 1870s. Miss Osburn remained head of nursing staff until 1884 and maintained a regular correspondence with Florence Nightingale until the latter died.

In 1876 the decrepit central wing of Macquarie's hospital was condemned and pulled down, and an architectural competition held for the design of a new hospital. Thomas Rowe won the first prize of £200 and by 1882 construction was well underway. The first floor was completed in 1884, when there was a change of government, the new government refusing to release further funds for completion of the building unless the hospital directors surrendered the hospital grounds as the government was anxious to acquire the site for a new Law Court. However there was another change of government with Sir Henry Parkes as Premier, who released funds to complete the building. The new Sydney Hospital finally opened in 1894, but with one less storey than originally planned to save money.

Tours of the hospital depart at 11.00am on Wednesdays from the lobby off the main Macquarie Street entrance.

Directly past the hospital on the left is the former *Mint,* located in the south wing of the old Rum Hospital.

The Old Mint
From the 17th to the 19th century, silver Spanish dollars – also known as pirates "pieces of eight", were

used as an international currency by the colonial trading nations.

Due to the disruption caused by European wars, there was a chronic shortage of currency circulating in the colony of New South Wales when Macquarie took over as Governor. To overcome the problem, in 1813 Macquarie converted 40,000 Spanish dollars into local coinage. A circular hole or "plug" was punched out of the centre of each dollar coin by William Hershell, a transported forger to make a dump worth 15 pence, while the remaining "holey dollar" retained its face value of five shillings. Both coins were counter-stamped "New South Wales 1813" on the obverse, with the denomination on the reverse. This was a shrewd move by Macquarie because Spanish dollars were worth four shillings and nine pence on the market at that time, so by inflating their value most of the coins remained in circulation on the local market as planned because trading ships wouldn't take them at face value in exchange for goods. The holey dollars and dumps remained in circulation until 1829, and are now much sought after by collectors.

When transportation of convicts ended in 1848 and convict patients were moved out of Sydney Hospital, the south wing became for a time *The Brigade Office* administering British army regiments serving in the colony of New South Wales. Following the gold rush which started in 1851, New South Wales authorities appealed to London for a Royal Mint to be established in Australia. The home authorities sent out the Royal Sappers and Miners Regiment in 1854 to convert the south wing of the Rum Hospital into a strongroom, offices and home for the Mint Master, while in the courtyard at the rear they built a "Melting House",

Coining Factory and Workshops out of prefabricated components they'd brought with them from England. The Coining Factory's prefabricated iron columns, girders and roofing were all similar in design to the components used in the Crystal Palace, London, built for the International Exhibition of 1851. The Royal Sappers and Miners had previously assisted in the erection of the Crystal Palace. The works supervisor wrote in 1854 during construction of the Coining Factory that he couldn't have found a better site, 'surrounded by a high wall... away from the public gaze, (it is) well adapted for erecting the manufactory'.

Two steam driven Taylor coin presses, manufactured by Joseph Taylor of Birmingham, England which could each produce 3,000 coins an hour were installed, and in 1855 they began striking their first gold sovereigns and half sovereigns. It was the first branch of the Royal Mint outside Britain. The presses had incredibly long working lives, one example still in the building, supplied to the Melbourne Mint in 1870 and identical to the type of machine supplied to the Sydney Mint in the 1850s, continued to be used for the production of coins and tokens until the early 1980s. Robert Hunt the first Deputy Mint Master, and Mint Assayer William Jevas, not finding the work "overly taxing" pursued other interests, including photography, and travelled New South Wales attempting to "attain perfection" in their images.

When the Mint closed in January 1927 the dilapidated buildings were saved from demolition because of a pressing need for government offices, and various government departments occupied the building until the 1970s when it was decided the Mint should be restored and

turned into a museum, which it remained as until 1997 when it was turned into a library and offices of the Historic Houses Trust.

Hyde Park Convict Barracks

On the corner of Macquarie Street and Prince Alfred Road stands *Hyde Park Barracks Museum*. During the early years of the colony, convicts labouring on public works were fed and clothed but not housed and either slept rough or begged for a place to sleep at night. With hundreds of convicts wandering the streets of Sydney every evening after work, crime was rampant. Macquarie had Francis Greenway design and build Hyde Park Convict Barracks (1817-1819), a three storey brick and sandstone dormitory to sleep 600 convicts. Opened on June 4, 1819 by Macquarie, the first 589 convicts staying in the barracks were served 'a most excellent dinner, plum pudding and an allowance of punch'. Following the sumptuous feast the convicts 'cheered His Excellency in reiterated peals'.

Convicts at the Barracks were required to work six days a week from sunrise to sunset, with a stop for lunch. On Sundays at Divine Service '... overseers... will impress on the men the importance of a decorous, attentive and devout demeanour...' '... on Sundays as well as every Thursday, the prisoners put on clean linen... hammocks are properly scrubbed at least once in every quarter, and... the blankets are washed every six months'. As the Chief Engineer wrote in 1819, 'Some (convicts) were pleased and these were the steady and best behaved who looked to it as a place of comfortable lodging and regular diet... there are others of more dissolute dispositions who regarded it as a place of restraint and still regard it as such'.

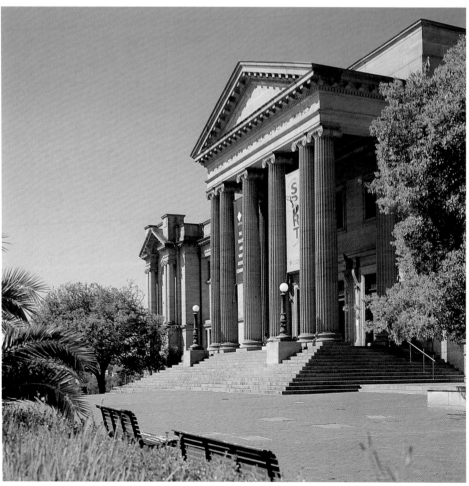

Clockwise from top left.

Sydney Hospital was designed by architect Thomas Rowe and completed in 1894. Rowe won the commission after receiving first prize in an architectural competition for the hospital, though some detractors criticised his architecture, labelling it as 'marked by a heavy hand... ponderous, leaden, even dull.' Thomas Rowe was also the first Mayor of Manly in 1877-78 and planted many of the Norfolk Island pines lining the beach promenades.

The modern wing of the State Library of New South Wales on Macquarie Street. The library has a good bookshop just off the south entrance, and a licensed restaurant, The Glasshouse Cafe on the same level as the General Reference Library reading room.

The Nightingale Wing of Sydney Hospital was built to house nursing teachers trained by Florence Nightingale.

Australia's first mint occupied the south wing of Macquarie's 'Rum Hospital'. When the building was first completed it was decorated to hold a ball to celebrate Napoleon's defeat at Waterloo when the news reached Australia in 1816. The Eastern "Chinoiserie" style of the first floor balcony railing matches Macquarie's original drawing for a 'Convict Hospital', and was put in place during restoration. The original slender Tuscan columns were turned by convicts from sandstone quarried

in the Domain. Heavily weathered and in an advanced state of deterioration, they were replaced with these new columns during restoration in 1978.

New South Wales Parliament House, Australia's oldest parliament. The State Legislative Council Chamber on the right is a pre-fabricated structure with a

framework of iron that was made in England, transported to Melbourne where it was used for housing, before being re-crated and moved to Sydney.

The Mitchell Wing of the State Library of New South Wales, contains, among many other things, the priceless Mitchell and Dixon collections, the biggest collection of

Australiana in the world. The library stands on the site of the "Female School of Industry", a former lighthorse barracks, which from 1826-70 taught domestic workers including reformed convicts 'every branch of household work'.

Previous page, (top), Hyde Park Barracks, "A Museum about itself", was a barracks for transported convicts. Commissioner Bigge wrote on Hyde Park Barracks in 1822, '... the leading object of security has been sacrificed to that of exhibiting with advantage and effect the regular proportion of the building' though he conceded 'The style of architecture... is simple and handsome, and the execution of the work is solid and promises to be durable...' A domed pavilion at the north west corner of the sandstone wall that encloses the barracks, the only remaining one of four that stood at each of the four corners, was once divided into five isolation cells for 'dissolute and refractory' convicts. It is now part of the Barrack's cafe.

The clock on Hyde Park Barracks (bottom left) completed in 1819, is Australia's oldest public clock. It was made by James Oatley, a convict clockmaker transported in 1815.

Victoria's statue, (bottom right) was unveiled before a large crowd during the Australian Centenary celebrations of 1888.

St James Church, (above), is the oldest in the City of Sydney. The church was originally designed as a courthouse (take away the spire and it looks like one) then Commissioner Bigge persuaded Macquarie it should be changed into a church. Bigge's brother-in-law, who travelled to New South Wales with him as his secretary, took up holy orders and was the first reverend of the church. The copper sheeting of the original spire was marked with broad arrows to identify it as government property in case of theft. A statue of Prince Albert, Victoria's husband, looks across to Victoria from his pedestal on the east (right) side of Macquarie Street.

Tuesday

The Manly Jetcat "Sea Eagle" off Admiralty House Kirribilli. There's nothing quite like a trip on the top deck of the Jetcat to blow away the cobwebs.

Manly Jetcat (right) passes the Opera House before arriving at Circular Quay.

Being in Hyde Park Barracks was not a punishment in itself, however prisoners were flogged for subsequent offences, the return from the Barracks in 1821 recording that during the year a total of 7,020 lashes were 'inflicted by order of the magistrates'. A convict, William Derrincourt recounted his own flogging at the barracks in the 1820s. '... if a man shouted out through pain he was looked upon as a sandstone or crawler. While the flogger was fixing me up he said to me quietly "Is there

any hangings to it" meaning had I anything to give him to lay the lash lightly. "Yes" I answered. "Allright" he said and then buckled to his work. The falls of the cat were enough to take my breath away and to draw my blood freely although comparatively lightly laid on..."

Inspectors frequently had to put up with insolence and abuse. In one incident on 11th August 1838 fifty men on a street gang went on strike after being asked to continue working past their normal knocking off time. Swinging at an inspector with a shovel and 'calling me "a bloody rotten scabby faced bugger" a bloody Negro-driving wretch (told the inspector) that "I worked the bloody guts out of the men and that they had better be hanged than placed under such a bloody tyrannising scabby faced dog as me."'

Discipline became tougher, the Reverend Sir Roger Therry recounting in the 1830s, '... As I passed along the road about eleven o'clock in the morning there issued out of the prisoners' barracks a party consisting of four men, who bore on their shoulders (two supporting the head and two the feet) a miserable convict, writhing in agony of pain – his voice piercing the air with terrific screams. Astonished at the site, I inquired what this meant, and was told it was "only a prisoner who had been flogged and was on his way to hospital." ... I soon learned that what I had seen was at that period an ordinary occurrence'.

Ernest Slade the Barracks' Superintendent wrote in 1833, 'The scourgers should be picked men of bodily height and power... at least two regular paid scourgers should

Tuesday

be appointed solely for the duty of Hyde Park Barracks, it being impossible for any scourger to duly administer more than 150 lashes in the course of one day'.

Slade's return of corporal punishments in September 1833 contained the following excerpts :

'Edward Scandrake Mangles, neglect of duty by feigning sickness, 25 lashes. He received 50 lashes last Monday week, but was never flogged before; his breech was sore from the last punishment; blood came at the first stroke; he screamed dreadfully at every lash; the blood running freely from the old wounds; he lost much blood; complained bitterly of the treatment...'

'William Smith Exmouth, drunk, insolent and resisting a constable, 50 lashes. This man was flogged about two years ago; he flinched much throughout the punishment; the skin was lacerated, and the blood appeared on the 24th lash; he seemed to suffer great pain, which was evinced by his suppressed groans; blood ran at the 45th lash, he cried out "domino" when finished'.

Slade thought that after a particular prisoner had received 50 lashes though he is '... known to be termed "flash" or "game"; nevertheless I am of the opinion that if all his former (or perhaps only his first) punishments had been as vigorously administered as this last, his indomitable spirit would have been subdued' and that after another 50 lashes '... suffered so severely

as to become, henceforth, more careful in subjecting himself to the infliction of punishment in Hyde Park Barrack under my superintendence.' Though even Slade wasn't completely without mercy, writing that a boy John Tree Asia, who received 36 lashes for feigning sickness '... suffered most severely ... in my opinion 12 lashes would have been sufficient ...'

When transportation ended the barracks became a hostel for single immigrant women, a home for old and destitute women, and finally Government departments and courts, before it was restored and reopened in 1984 as a museum. Following its conversion for use by the courts the interior of the Barracks was subdivided into Judges' chambers, rooms for witnesses, records and administration, including a large room for "lunacy clerks" looking after the paperwork for an adjoining "Lunacy Court".

Among a variety of fascinating displays is a room on the archaeology of the barracks, another with models depicting changes at the site, a hands on convict data base (perhaps to trace your convict background), and reconstructed convict dormitories with rough hewn timber frames supporting rows of canvas hammocks. Put your feet up for five minutes, swing on a hammock and listen to the tape recording about living conditions for convicts in the barracks. The Barracks are open seven days a week, 10.00am to 5.00pm except Christmas Day and Good Friday.

St. James Church

Cross Macquarie Street to *St. James Church* (1819-1822), directly opposite the barracks. St. James was designed originally as a courtroom by Francis Greenway, then Macquarie asked Greenway to change his plans to turn it into a church. Inside the church the fine craftsmanship of the polished marble railing and mosaic floor of the sanctuary make a striking contrast to the relative plainness of the rest of the interior.

One of the Manly Ferries (left). Ferries have been part of everyday life in Sydney since the earliest days of the colony, when a punt ran from Sydney Cove to Parramatta. These days, over 10,000 people a day commute to work on ferries. Sydney has the second busiest network of ferries in the world after Hong Kong.

The Manly Ferry arriving at Manly Cove (above).

Boxing Day crowds at South Steyne, Manly Beach (right).

A big summer surf rolling in on Manly Beach (right).

Queenscliff at the north end of Manly Beach (right).

A surf carnival at Manly Beach (right page top).

The Corso (right page bottom) dates to the 1850s when Henry Gilbert Smith cleared the bush for a distance of 400 metres between Manly Wharf and the Ocean Beach. Smith called his new street 'The Corso' after the ancient street in Rome.

47

Memorial plaques inside the church include one to Commodore James Brisbane, Commander of the British naval force during the Burmese War. To recuperate from sickness resulting from the arduous campaign Brisbane landed in Sydney, but never recovered and died in December 1826. Three other separate memorials fixed to the walls of the church are to a soldier, settler and explorer killed by aborigines in different parts of Australia in the early nineteenth century. Convicts from the Hyde Park Barracks were marched across for Sunday service to a separate entrance and gallery of the church with '… their best clothes well brushed, their hands and faces washed and their shoes cleaned'.

Francis Greenway's *Supreme Court Building*, directly behind the church,

still functions as a sheriff's office and has four working courts. A door outside St. James Church on the west side of the steeple facing the Supreme Court, leads to the brick vaulted church crypt, possibly intended to be used as cells if the church had fulfilled its original function as a court. One of the chambers in the crypt, contains a childrens' chapel with frescoes of scenes from the bible transposed to Australian settings.

The Supreme Court

On the same side of Macquarie Street next to *St. James Church*, is the modern New South Wales Supreme Court building, containing 40 courts including arbitration courts, federal courts and supreme courts. Its showpiece, the amphitheatred *Banco Court*, on the 13th level, can be

viewed from the press gallery when the court is in session. One floor further up at the top of the building, the *Law Courts' Restaurant* is open to the public. The coffee lounge, open from 7.00am to 3.30pm, serves breakfast and snacks and the restaurant, open 11.30am to 2.00pm serves reasonably priced meals with no charge for the fantastic view of Hyde Park, Macquarie Street and the Botanical Gardens.

On the forecourt in front of St. James Church near Macquarie Street, go down the steps leading to *St. James underground station* and catch a train one stop to Circular Quay. While you are waiting for your train at St. James you will have time to admire the splendour of the station's original 1920's colour scheme of cream and green tiles.

Previous pages : Aerial view of Manly.

Unspoilt Collins Beach at Manly (left) is the site where Governor Phillip was speared and wounded by an aborigine. Phillip, who insisted his men were not to retaliate, made a

full recovery after six weeks' rest.

The white sand of Shelly Beach (bottom left) is made up of granules of millions of finely ground sea shells. It is one of only two west facing beaches on the east coast of Australia.

A hospital and disinfection buildings stand close to the beach at the Manly Quarantine Station (below). The one mile wide entry passage to Sydney Harbour is in the background.

General Macarthur had his Sydney wartime headquarters in a disused railway tunnel at the station.

Circular Quay

At *Circular Quay* pick up a free copy of the timetable of Sydney ferries and jetcats with connecting bus services, from the Ferry Information Counter. During the week ferries and jetcats to *Manly* run about every half hour.

Ferries are to Sydney what gondolas are to Venice, they are part of everyday life and thousands of people commute to work on them daily. While you are on your way out to Manly, bear in mind the motto of the Port Jackson Steam Ship Company formed in 1881, that ran the Manly Ferries 'Four pence spent on a trip to Manly is better than a

pound on medicine'. Jetcats to Manly leave from No.2 Jetty, Manly Ferries leave from No.3 Jetty, at Circular Quay. The faster jetcats are slightly more expensive than the ferries, and have no half fares for children.

Manly

After entering Sydney Harbour on January 21, 1788 and spending the night at Camp Cove, Phillip's longboats started exploring the harbour shoreline the following morning. According to Phillip's dispatches to England, on January 22, 1788:

'The boats in passing near a point of land in the harbour were seen by a number of men and 20 of them waded into the water unarmed, received what was offered to them and examined the boats with a

curiosity that gave me a much higher opinion of them… and their confidence and manly bearing made me give the name Manly Cove to this place'.

The following day Phillip went on to discover and name Sydney Cove.

Manly remained an area of sparsely populated bushland until the 1850s, when *Henry Gilbert Smith*, inspired by Brighton from his native Sussex in England, developed 120 acres of land he owned in Manly. Smith erected a ferry wharf at Manly Cove, built a hotel nearby and cleared the bush from the wharf through to the ocean beach 500 metres away, to form a road he called *'The Corso'* after a street in Rome. With tents where refreshments were served, a public bathhouse, maze, gardens, swings, walks

Manly Jetcat departing Manly Wharf (right).

and a ferry service to bring day-trippers from Sydney, Smith had turned Manly into a resort 60 years before Bondi became popular.

Strange as it may seem, public bathing was banned at this time in Manly in view of a public place, between 6.00am and 8.00pm. William Gocher, the Editor of the Manly and North Shore News, announced in his paper in October 1902 that he would bathe in daylight hours and damn the consequences. Gocher was arrested, but a local Magistrate wouldn't fine him and following further campaigning the law was repealed in November 1903. That year the Sly brothers started Australia's first Life Saving Service at Manly, operating from an old fishing boat and Sydney's beach and swimming tradition was born.

There's plenty to do in Manly. A good start would be to walk through The Corso to *Manly Visitors Information Bureau* on the promenade, to pick up a free map of Manly with locations of places of interest and a shopping guide.

Walks
Easy walks following oceanside and harbourside tracks lead to parks, bushland and beaches. From the ferry wharf turn left along West Esplanade past *Manly Museum* and *Oceanworld* to a waterside path that follows the harbour foreshore past *Fairlight Beach* to a park at North Harbour. Or, turn right at the Ferry Wharf along East Esplanade to Stuart Street, walk the length of Stuart Street past *Little Manly Cove* and turn left at the end to follow a foreshore track leading, after about five minutes walk, to *Spring Cove Beach* surrounded by natural bushland. On September 7, 1790, Governor Phillip was speared through the shoulder by an aborigine when he stepped ashore at Spring Cove, searching for an aborigine who had been captured earlier at Manly, held

at Sydney and later escaped. Phillip, who insisted that his men were not to retaliate, made a full recovery after six weeks rest.

From Manly Wharf a bus service runs four kilometres to *North Head Lookout* on top of the cliffs at the north entrance to Sydney Harbour. On the way the bus passes the entrance to the *Quarantine Station*. Immigrant ships entering Sydney carrying passengers infected by contagious diseases, stopped at the Quarantine Station for six weeks while all passengers and crew went through quarantine procedures. The station is administered by the National Parks and Wildlife Service and to go on one of their guided tours you need to book in advance by phoning the service.

From the south end of Manly Ocean Beach, a 20 minute walk on Marine Parade leads to *Shelly Beach*. With a view looking back onto Manly Beach, Shelly Beach is one of only two west facing beaches on the east coast of Australia.

A useful alternative to a walk or a tour, particularly if it's a hot day, is to find a patch of sand and simply relax on the beach for a few hours. That should be enough to work up a thirst ready for quenching in one of the bars on The Corso or in the Manly Pacific Park Royal Hotel.

Tonight, why not leaf through your brochure from Manly Tourist Promotions to choose a restaurant for your evening meal, before taking the Manly Ferry back to Circular Quay. The choice of restaurants in Manly covers the gamut of international cuisine, with prices to suit all pockets from the five star Manly Pacific Park Royal to The Corso take-aways. For excellent seafood and relaxing water views, Le Kiosk at Shelly Beach is up market but good, or for the budget traveller Manly Wharf shops has a variety of cafes and restaurants.

The cliffs of North Head (above) with the entrance of Sydney Harbour in the background. The Sydney Harbour shoreline including the Parramatta and Lane Cove Rivers is 250 kilometres long and encloses 55 square kilometres of water.

The quiet cloisters of Manly Seminary (right) now house the International College of Tourism and Hotel Management.

Tuesday

WEDNESDAY

Wednesday

Sydney bushland and the Northern Beaches

Following a stroll in the morning taking in some of the last and grandest buildings of the colonial period built in Sydney, then a drive to the sprawling Ku-ring-gai Chase National Park, 50 kilometres to the north, we finish the day with a visit in the evening to the bars and nightclubs of the Leicester Square of Sydney, Kings Cross.

Start at Wharf Four at Circular Quay. Sydney Ferries run an excellent information counter on the corner opposite the wharf beneath Circular Quay Station. Just around the corner, opposite the *Paragon Hotel*, the N.S.W. Government runs a travel centre providing free information on the 'Seven Wonders of New South Wales' and how to get there and where to stay. Cross Alfred Street at the traffic lights to the First Fleet Memorial (1980). The Memorial, of two bulbous copper links set on a granite plinth, looks like a pair of entwined aircraft tyre inner-tubes. The sculpture, titled "Bonds of Friendship", the granite base of which was quarried from Dartmoor, England, is a companion piece to

one erected near the Sally Port at Portsmouth through which many of the First Fleeters passed on their way to embark on the First Fleet. The links in the chain symbolise the bonds of friendship forged between Sydney and Portsmouth that resulted from the sailing of the fleet. The plinth of the Portsmouth monument is cut from a block of New South Wales granite.

Directly in front of the First Fleet Memorial is the *Customs House*, which has the names on scrolls of various outposts of the British Empire decorating the facade. The Customs House grew with the times. The original two storey building, completed in 1845, was partially dismantled and rebuilt to three storeys in 1885. Several further alterations and additions, completed in 1903, saw the building emerge as a five storey structure, then finally a six storey structure in 1917 when a caretaker's quarters was built on top. The imposing facade of the Customs House makes an

Previous pages : Middle Harbour and the Spit Bridge. Sir Thomas Mitchell explorer (left) one of the prominent figures from early New South Wales colonial days whose statues decorate the facade of the Lands Department Building on Bridge Street. A wooden bridge, erected October 1788 (the first in the colony) and replaced by a stone bridge 1803-4, stood near the corner of Bridge and Pitt Streets.

Circular Quay and the City (below left).

Macquarie Place (below), packed with office workers eating their lunch on weekdays, is deserted at the same time on a Saturday. The anchor and a cannon from the 'Sirius', flagship of the First Fleet, are on the right. Francis Greenway's obelisk to mark road distances in New South Wales, erected 1818, is on the left near the steps. Sydney's first streetlight, burning whale oil, was erected in the park in 1826. The original facade and marble bar of the Customs House Hotel on the north west side of Macquarie Place, have been incorporated into the Ramada Renaissance Hotel.

Wednesday

Clockwise from top left : The lion and the unicorn on the Customs House, the spectacular pointed top of 1 O'Connell Street, the foyer of Governor Phillip Tower and the onion domed clock tower of the Lands Department Building. Note the observatory dome in front of the clock tower.

Clockwise from top left : Statue of Victoria gracing the G.P.O. "cover your breast mistress", the Cenotaph on 11th November, the clock tower of the G.P.O. and the Museum of Sydney backed by the massive structure of Governor Phillip Tower. The lost office space in the negative detailing of the tower will cost the developers millions over the life of the building.

uplifting contrast to the Stalinist facade of *Circular Quay Railway Station* on the opposite side of Alfred Street. According to a notice on the Australian Customs Service at the front of the Customs House '… Customs Officers (have) patrolled the docks to protect citizens from illegal activities; apprehended smugglers and intercepted the importation of contraband; illicit drugs; dangerous weapons and the like – without fear or favour… The safety of Australians today, the independence of our economy and the regard with which the world holds our nation, is due in no small way to the dedication and diligence of Customs Officers'.

Turn right, then left up Loftus Street, following the outside wall of the Customs House. After a few metres you pass a Union Flag hanging on a flagpole set in the pavement. A Committee of Enquiry appointed by Sydney Council in 1963 examined historical evidence and concluded that this was close to the spot where Phillip raised the Union Flag on January 26, 1788. Early in the morning on that date, 26 officers and marines stepped ashore at Sydney Cove from the First Fleet, raised the Union Flag (forbearer of the Union Jack), fired four volleys of small arms and drank a toast to the new colony.

Macquarie Place

A little further up Loftus Street is the small park at *Macquarie Place*, a shady haven not much bigger than the average suburban garden. The park was set aside originally by Governor Macquarie from part of the garden of Old Government House. The flagship of the First Fleet, an old frigate that had served in the American War of Independence and was renamed the *Sirius* for its new mission after the brightest star in the southern sky, sank off Norfolk Island in March 1790 while on a journey to China for supplies. The anchor from the *Sirius* and one of its cannons, recovered in 1907, can be found in the park. A sandstone obelisk nearby, designed by Francis Greenway and erected in 1818, is the benchmark for road distances from Sydney to the rest of Australia. Two trees at the south east corner of the park were planted by the Queen and Prince Phillip to mark the start of their "Remembrance Driveway" to Canberra on 5th February, 1954.

Pass the statue of the great Australian pioneer, Thomas Sutcliffe Mort at the south west corner of the park and cross to the Lands Department Building on the corner of Bridge and Gresham Streets. The Lands Department was built over a period of 20 years from the 1870s to the 1890s. A stately onion domed clock tower and an observatory (which was never used) grace the roof. Forty eight niches in the outside walls of the Lands Department contain some statues of Australian explorers and legislators. Twenty five niches were left unfilled when the building was completed, and they have remained vacant ever since. Have there been no explorers or legislators since deemed worthy of occupying the places?

Walk round the exterior of the Lands Department building along Gresham Street, then turn left on Bent Street. The street's irregular course once skirted the vegetable garden of Old Government House. Rearing high on the opposite side of the road is No 1 O'Connell Street, the pointed top of which made a spectacular addition to the city skyline when it was completed in 1991. The top can only be seen from further up Bent Street. The Wintergarden shopping plaza on the O'Connell Street, Bent Street and Spring Street levels is a useful location for a coffee or a bite to eat.

Cross Loftus Street to the Education Department building (1913) on Farrer Place. If art deco is your pecko, make sure to stroll 100 metres down O'Connell Street to Delfin House (1940) at No.16, designed by Bruce Dellit. Looking at the exterior and bronze doors of Delfin House one wonders where art finishes and architecture starts.

Cross Farrer Place ascend the steps and pass through the revolving doors to the foyer of Governor Phillip Tower (1993). The lofty foyer of Governor Phillip Tower and the adjoining Governor Macquarie Tower are like something out of the dying days of the Holy Roman Empire. The Romans though, lacked the technology to produce the superb craftsmanship in stainless steel. Extraordinary bronze sculptures of Phillip and Macquarie grace the respective foyers. Walk to the north east corner of the courtyard cafe off the foyer and crane your neck to look up to the top of the Tower. The pattern of stainless steel bars on the exterior creates an optical illusion so the square top of the building looks curved. Re-enter the foyer and walk up the steps and through the doors to Phillip Street. Turn left past a row of five terraced houses – one of the few survivors of the housing that used to grace much of the inner-city – to the *Museum of Sydney*.

Museum of Sydney

The Museum of Sydney stands on the spot where a portable canvas structure carried on one of the First Fleet ships was erected as the first Governor's House. In May 1788 construction commenced on a permanent Government House built in Georgian style from locally made bricks. This building was demolished without ceremony in 1845, and all that remains are some of the foundations which can be seen through glass panels in the floor of the foyer of the Museum. The most dramatic event to take place at old Government House occurred during the Sydney Rum Rebellion of 1808. The hapless Governor Bligh, who, following the Mutiny on the Botany enjoyed a short term as Governor of N.S.W., was deposed by a mutiny on land during the rebellion. Nearby Bligh street is named after the Governor. Bligh described in a letter to his friend Joseph Banks how '… This rebellious act was done so suddenly that in about five minutes from the time we first knew of it, Government House was surrounded with troops, Major Johnstone having brought up in battle array above three hundred men under martial law, loaded with ball to attack and seize my person and a few friends... that had been at dinner with me... they marched to the tune of the 'British Grenadiers', and to render the spectacle more terrific to the townspeople, the field artillery... was presented against the house...'

Every museum contains its own particular treasures and the Museum of Sydney is no exception. There are displays of aboriginal artefacts which once belonged to the Eora aboriginal people who inhabited Sydney before the white feller. Behind glass in the foyer is the original Government House foundation plate, laid by Governor Phillip on 15th May 1788 and uncovered quite by chance by Bob McCann, a telegraph lines worker in 1899. Inside the museum is an entire jib crane with a cast-iron frame and gears that used to perch on the wharf next to Campbell's Store in the Rocks. Upstairs in a large glass case is Governor Bligh's sword and a locally carved seat that once belonged to Governor Macquarie. Upholstered with wallaby fur and with a back capped with a wooden hand clutching a dagger, the seat looks more like something out of the banqueting hall of a Scottish castle than a seat of a Governor in the antipodes. Don't miss the magical visuals in the "Bond Store".

Chifley Tower

Backtrack up Phillip Street to Chifley Tower on the south east corner of Bent Street. This building is a monument to the final days of the Holy Alan Bond Empire. The building was designed and planned and construction had got underway when Bond's business empire collapsed. However, construction was completed by new owners. The building, clad in pink granite and white marble flecked with black grain, does have a certain style about it, and without the entrepreneurship of people like Bond, buildings like this wouldn't happen – though whether the Bond Corporation shareholders would agree is another matter.

Walk up the steps and through the doors into the entry hall, and right into the lobby past a remarkable sculpture "Night Sea Crossing 1992" by Akio Makigawa. A lift can take you to the *Forty One Restaurant* on Level 41, though you certainly would have needed to book if you're planning on stopping for lunch. The restaurant, on two levels connected by a sweeping staircase, has superb views of the harbour and eastern Sydney and the excellent food prepared by a dedicated staff is very good value. Bond had planned to use the location for his Sydney penthouse if his fortunes hadn't taken a nose-dive.

Return to the lobby and walk through to Chifley Plaza shops. Beautiful mosaics of Australian flowers are inset into the floor of the food court on the top level of the plaza. Leave the plaza by the main entrance on the ground floor to Chifley Square, named after Ben Chifley, the locomotive engine driver who became Australian Prime Minister.

Across Chifley Square on the ground floor of the Goodsell Building on the corner of Elizabeth Street and Hunter Street is the *Government Information Service of N.S.W.* The Service offers free information on all aspects of N.S.W. Government and has a range of Government products for sale, including maps and Acts of Parliament. Walk up Elizabeth Street to the State Bank of N.S.W. on the corner of Martin Place. The bank has a cavernous beige marble foyer, with seven galleries rising to a glass skylight.

Martin Place

In Martin Place on the west side of Elizabeth Street is the *Half Tix Kiosk*, where half price tickets to selected Sydney shows and concerts are available on the day of purchase between noon and 6.00pm. Free tourist information and maps are available in the adjoining Sydney Convention and Visitors' Bureau Kiosk.

On Martin Place next to the kiosk is the banking hall of the *Commonwealth Bank* at number 48, the ceiling of which is supported by a grove of green marble columns. A white marble lobby, entry and staircase, with a stained glass barrel-vault ceiling, opening to the north of the banking hall, is something just wonderful.

Walk a short distance down Martin Place and turn right at Castlereagh Street, the next street down. One hundred metres along at No. 9 is the *Capita Building*. As you walk through the entry courtyard look up to the roof, which soars 65 metres above. The bold blue, white and silver design in tiles on the west wall of the entry is by Lin Utzon, daughter of Sydney Opera House Architect Jorn Utzon. The courtyard leads into the Atrium Restaurant, a good place to rest your feet and have a coffee, or return another time for a meal. While on the subject of architecture, make sure to see the bronze sculpture above the entrance to the art deco style *City Mutual Building* nearby on the corner of Bligh and Hunter Streets.

Backtrack along Castlereagh Street and continue down the pedestrian mall of Martin Place. At the amphi-theatre in the centre, lunchtime crowds enjoy free shows ranging from sheep shearing displays to ethnic dance groups and live rock bands. Pass the *Dobell Memorial Sculpture*, (1979), an erection of stainless steel pyramids one on top of the other known locally as the 'Silver Shish Kebab' and cross Pitt Street to James Barnet's *G.P.O. building*.

When construction of the G.P.O. was commenced in 1866 by Government Architect James Barnet,

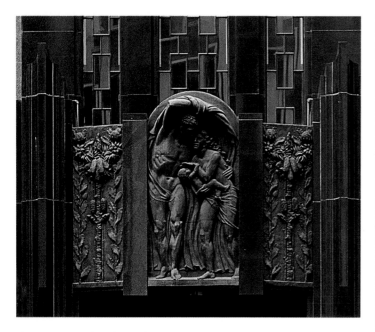

Awesome art-deco (above) on the City Mutual Building.

The entry to the Capital building (right) on Castlereagh Street.

Sydney's two most spectacular cable-stayed structures (far right) the Glebe Island Bridge and Sydney Tower.

Australia's postal services had advanced remarkably since the appointment of Australia's first postmaster in 1809. That year Isaac Nichols Esquire; transported for stealing a donkey, started a post office at his own home. The G.P.O. was completed in stages and opened for the colony's centenary in 1887. One of the main attractions for the first users of the Post Office was the opportunity to ride in Sydney's first lifts. The clock wasn't finally fitted to the clock tower until 1891. In 1942 the Sydney Council, concerned that the 64 metre high G.P.O. clock tower may be used as a reference point by Japanese pilots to bomb the centre of Sydney, dismantled the tower and put the pieces in storage. The tower stayed down for over 20 years until it was dusted off and re-erected in 1963.

For 100 years everyone was quite happy to buy stamps and post letters in the G.P.O. then Australia Post, in their wisdom, decided to move the G.P.O. round the corner into more modern premises at 157-171 Pitt Street. James Barnet would have turned in his grave. However the building and clock tower remain as one of the greatest monuments of the late colonial period built in Sydney.

In Martin Place opposite the G.P.O. on the site where the first recruiting office stood during the First World War, stands the *Cenotaph* where a dawn service is held every Anzac Day and a memorial service every Remembrance Day at 11.00am on November 11th. Stop for a while to ponder the message "Lest We Forget", inscribed on the side of the Cenotaph. Australia suffered tremendous losses in both World Wars, and casualties in the Malayan Emergency and Vietnam. A memorial service played by members of the 2nd Military District Brass Band takes place at the Cenotaph every Thursday at 12.30pm.

George Street

At the junction of Martin Place and George Street, several banks and insurance companies have their head offices. Constructed at the turn of the century and early this century, the buildings are styled in typical 'solid as a rock' fashion of the period, with polished marble and granite predominating. On a wet Sydney winter's day, when commuters with umbrellas raised are hurrying between rain squalls, squint your eyes and try to tell yourself that you're not in the City of London. One of these temples of finance is the National Australia Bank at 343 George Street, while the banking hall of the Royal Bank across the road at the corner of 354 George Street in the former Bank of Australasia building (1908) is a veritable Versailles.

Turning right down George Street the High Street of Governor Phillip's Sydney renamed George Street by Governor Macquarie after George III, pass *Australia Square* Tower on the

right. Good views of Sydney can be enjoyed from the revolving *Summit Restaurant* at the top.

A little further along George Street at the junction of Essex Street, is the site of Sydney's first gaol. Public hangings here were a popular entertainment of the day. A plaque on the *Regent Hotel* , at the corner of Essex and Harrington Streets, cheerfully announces 'The First Fleet Execution. Thomas Barrett, a First Fleet convict was hanged near this place on February 27, 1788 for stealing provisions and was buried nearby.'. On a less sombre note, the cafe in the Regent Hotel is an excellent place to rest your feet and enjoy a coffee and a bite to eat.

Last but not least; continuing on George Street and under the Cahill Expressway, a minute or so's walk brings you to James Barnet's *Rocks Police Station* (1882). Note the lion holding a baton in its mouth on the keystone above the entrance. The police station is built on the site of the First Fleet Hospital, a crude structure thrown together from branches, bark and wattle, to house the sick when the First Fleet landed.

The Docks

Assuming you have managed to beg, borrow or steal a car, continue in motorised fashion in a northerly direction on George Street and turn right into *Hickson Road*. In 1900, 113 people died of the plague in Sydney, mostly in The Rocks. Rats from ships at nearby Walsh Bay spread the disease and the Sydney Harbour Trust was formed in 1901 to clear up The Rocks and prevent another outbreak occurring. The Trust resumed ownership of private wharves running from Walsh Bay to Darling Harbour, quarantined the area and the Trust's first President, Robert Hickson, demolished houses and warehouses to build a 30 metre wide road around the waterfront, enclosed on the landward side by a high rat proof wall. In a bacteriological laboratory set up on nearby Goat Island, Dr Frank Tidswell proved by experimenting (for the first time) that it was the fleas carried by rats that spread bubonic plague, and not the rats themselves.

Follow Hickson Road under the Harbour Bridge and past Pier One. Pier 4, houses the Wharf Theatre and Restaurant. The theatre, opened in 1984, is currently leased by the Sydney Theatre Company. There are conducted tours which give a history of the wharf and theatre and take visitors backstage and to the rehearsal rooms.

Continue on Hickson Road past Darling Harbour docks on the right and Napoleon's Hotel on the left into Sussex Street. Turn right at Market Street just before the overhead monorail track at the signpost for Pyrmont and Glebe. By a little careful traffic negotiation on the freeway, keep to the left to get onto the elevated expressway over Darling Harbour and follow the signs for the Fish Markets. After two kilometres drive stop at the Fish

Fig Tree Bridge and Gladesville Bridge (right). The peninsular of Hunters Hill is on the left.

Marinas on Pittwater at Newport (below).

Markets car park – fish markets smell the same wherever you go. Stroll to the Waterfront Arcade shops. Inspecting the great variety of sea creatures on display is as much fun as a visit to the Sydney Aquarium, but at least at the Fish Markets you can eat them! Giant Tasmanian crabs with claws up to 25cms long are sold by weight for up to $200. Mum would love you to take one home to keep in the bath. Abalone shells 15cm long reflecting all the colours of the rainbow can be bought for 50¢ each to go in the bath to keep the crab happy. Or failing that, they make a neat soap dish. For a budget priced lunch, go for the "Workers Box" at Peter's Fish-market, if you're not ravenous it's enough for two. Take your meal box outside to eat on one of the tables at the quayside overlooking the fishing boats on *Blackwattle Bay*.

Leave the Fish Markets and follow the signs for Ryde and Victoria Road to get onto the *Glebe Island Bridge*. The bridge is as big a folly as the Sydney Opera House, even bigger in fact, because it's longer, higher and cost more to build. At least at the Opera House you can watch an opera – all the Glebe Island Bridge does is carry traffic. The enormous span of the bridge was built to replace the narrow opening of the former Glebe Island Swing Bridge, and the great height of the span so shipping could enter Blackwattle Bay and Rozelle Bay. But ships almost never enter the enclosed water of the bay, why didn't the

Government fill the bay in for a park with a lake or waterfront housing and just build a road across Glebe Island. But if they'd done that we wouldn't have the sculptural cable-stayed Glebe Island Bridge to distract us on the way to Victoria Road.

Glebe Island, these days joined to the suburb of Rozelle by land reclamations, was the site of the Sydney Abattoirs from 1852 to early in the twentieth century. These days the island is host to massive grain han-

dling silos and a busy container ship terminal. Two kilometres past Glebe Island Bridge, turn right onto Victoria Road.

Passing through the suburbs of *Rozelle* and *Drummoyne*, crossing *Iron Cove Bridge* (1954) and negotiating 13 sets of traffic lights on the way, go up and over the graceful arch of *Gladesville Bridge*. The bridge's 305 metre span was the longest concrete arch span in the world when it was completed in October 1964. The Gladesville Bridge replaced an old

The view of Barrenjoey Headland (top), from Commodore Heights at West Head.

West Head Road (above left) in Ku-ring-gai Chase National Park. The park covers 14,712 hectares of bushland on the north east outskirts of Sydney. Planners set aside the area, only 24 km north of Sydney, in 1894. The sandstone plateau of the park, dissected by scenic waterways, is well known for its Aboriginal carvings, wild flowers, bush walks and picnic areas.

McCarr's Creek Road (above) winds through unspoilt bush.

Wednesday

swing bridge opened in February 1881, which was the first bridge spanning the main channel of Sydney Harbour. The swing bridge in turn replaced the so-called Bedlam Ferry, crossing the Parramatta River two kilometres to the west at the Great North Road. The ferry received its name because of the nearby location of Gladesville Mental Hospital. In fact the point on the north shore of the river from where the ferries used to leave has been called Bedlam Point ever since.

Houses at Hunters Hill

As the road forks coming down from Gladesville Bridge, take the right fork signposted for *Lane Cove*, then a short distance later turn off the highway following the signposts for *Hunters Hill*. Follow Church Street, Alexandra Street and Woolwich Road to *Clarke Reserve*, a grassy park on the water-front at Clarke's Point with good views of the harbour. The *Woolwich Pier Hotel* (1892) at the end of Woolwich Road; with its bar and bistro, a good spot to stop for a bite

Tame kookaburras at West Head (top left).

Houses at Church Point on Pittwater (top right).

Warriewood and Mona Vale Beach (above). At low tide you can walk around the rocks from Warriewood to Mona Vale beach.

Narrabeen Lakes (above) with Narrabeen Beach and the Pacific Ocean in the background. Narrabeen Head, North Narrabeen Beach and the road bridge at Ocean Street over Narrabeen Lake (left).

The five kilometre sweep of Collaroy and Narrabeen Beach (below left).

Long Reef Beach and Long Reef Point (below) are a protected Aquatic Reserve.

Freshwater Beach (above) with Manly and North Head in the background. Mounted on a rock in the centre of the headland on the left is a bronze statue on a surfboard of the Hawaiian swimmer and surfer Duke Kahanamoku. The Duke introduced surfing to Australia when he gave a demonstration of his surfboard riding skills at Harbord Beach (now known as Freshwater Beach) in December 1914. At the adjoining Duke Kahanamoku Commemorative Park, plaques on "The Mosaic Walk" feature Australian men and women who since 1964 have held Long and Short Board Surfing World Championships. Duke Kahanamoku was the first man to swim 100 yards in under one minute, broke the 50 metres and 100 metres freestyle world records on several occasions, and won medals at the 1912 Stockholm, 1920 Antwerp, 1924 Paris and 1932 (at the age of 42) Los Angeles Olympics. Between 1920 and the 1950s he starred in about 30 Hollywood movies with actors such as Henry Fonda, John Wayne and Ronald Colman, and from 1934-1960 served as an elected Sheriff of Honolulu.

Dee Why and Dee Why Lagoon, above right. James Meahan, the surveyor, a reformed convict, one of the first explorers of the area who drew the first maps, wrote on the bottom corner of his map of one of the beaches the letters D.Y. In his diary notes made during the journey, Meahan wrote that the area was covered with thick bush and hard to reach. Later scholars referring back through his diaries thought the letters D.Y. on the map may be short for the Greek Dyspropositas, meaning not easy to find and hard to reach.

Curl Curl rock pool and Curl Curl beach (above).

of lunch, enjoys a view straight down the harbour to the Harbour Bridge from the first floor.

The picturesque, charming suburb of Hunters Hill owes its existence to the French brothers Didier and Jules Joubert, who emigrated to Sydney in the 1840s, bought 200 acres of land at Hunters Hill, subdivided it and with 40 stonemasons they brought out from Italy, built elegant homes from locally quarried sandstone. The suburb has changed very little since the houses were finished, most of the 200 or so homes built by the Joubert brothers are still standing.

Ku-ring-gai Chase

Backtrack through Hunters Hill to rejoin the main road, follow Burns Bay Road and Centennial Avenue to Epping Road, turn right at the traffic lights at Epping Road then left three kilometres later at the traffic lights at the *Pacific Highway*. Follow the Pacific Highway through the suburbs of Roseville, Lindfield, Killara and Gordon, then turn right

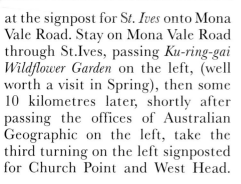

The Spit Bridge at Middle Harbour (left) receives its name because of the sandspit on the south side of the bridge. For 38 years, from 1850 to 1888, a man called Ellery worked the crossing with a hand punt. Many Sydney residents can still remember when the crossing was serviced by a cable ferry before the first bridge was built in 1924.

The present Spit Bridge with a single lift span dates from 1959. At Clontarf Park behind the beach on the left of the picture, an Irishman, H.J. O'Farrell shot and wounded Prince Alfred, Duke of Edinburgh, son of Queen Victoria in 1868 while he was having a picnic there. O'Farrell was hanged for his trouble.

Long traffic queues form when the Spit Bridge (top) lifts several times a day to allow yachts and ferries to pass.

Boronia House 1885 (above) on Military Road Mosman, for many years the local library, is now a restaurant.

at the signpost for S*t. Ives* onto Mona Vale Road. Stay on Mona Vale Road through St.Ives, passing *Ku-ring-gai Wildflower Garden* on the left, (well worth a visit in Spring), then some 10 kilometres later, shortly after passing the offices of Australian Geographic on the left, take the third turning on the left signposted for Church Point and West Head.

Tunnels, storehouses and gunpits at Middle Head (right) are the most extensive old system of defence works on Sydney Harbour. Many of the passages, tunnels, pits and stairs are chiselled directly out of the sandstone of the head.

Balmoral Beach (right) is the longest of the Sydney Harbour beaches.

Following page : William Street at dusk (top left). The Hyatt Kingsgate Hotel, at the top of the street, has a view from the rooms of the Sydney city skyline.

The El Alamein Fountain Kings Cross (top right) commemorates the men of the Australian Ninth Division who fought in North Africa during the Second World War.

The "world famous" Pink Pussycat (below right). Say no more.

Trains are usually the last thing on the minds of visitors to Kings Cross (bottom left).

And so is Coca-Cola. The illuminated Coca-Cola sign on Darlinghurst Road at Kings Cross (centre left).

Seven Days

73

The road soon enters bushland and becomes quite winding as it passes through stands of eucalyptus trees. Keep following the sign-posts for West Head, turning left over the bridge over McCarr's Creek to the entrance to the National Park. There is an entry charge per car. At the kiosk, at the entrance, the National Parks and Wildlife Officer on duty will be pleased to give you free pamphlets covering walks and tours, the location of aboriginal carvings and general information about *Ku-ring-gai Chase National Park*.

Stunning Views

Once past the kiosk, after a short distance turn right onto the road for *West Head* and follow it for 12 kilometres as it traverses a high sandstone bush covered plateau to *Commodore Heights Lookout* on the tip of West Head. From this point you can enjoy one of the best scenic views to be found around Sydney, with panoramas of Pittwater, the Warringah Peninsular and Palm Beach to the south and east and Broken Bay, Lion Island Nature Reserve, Brisbane Water National Park and Bouddi National Park to the north. Tame kookaburras that will eat from your hand make an amusing diversion at West Head if you tire of the views.

Returning by the same route to McCarr's Creek Road, follow it in an easterly direction as it skirts the picturesque suburb of *Church Point* on the shore of *Pittwater*. When Governor Phillip explored the area in March 1788, he noted that Pittwater was "The finest piece of water I ever saw", and named it after the British Prime Minister Pitt the Younger.

Beaches Galore

Turn right at the traffic lights at Mona Vale to join the three lane highway of Pittwater Road; then after passing Mona Vale Golf Course on the left, turn left onto Coronation Street. Pass Mona Vale Hospital and keeping to the left, follow the road around the top of the headland past

the small beaches of *Warriewood* and *Turimetta*, pass a caravan and camping ground on the right, over the bridge at the entrance to *Narrabeen Lakes* and into Ocean Street. The street follows the long five kilometre curve of *Narrabeen* and *Collaroy Beaches*. They are in fact one long beach, (the northern end is Narrabeen) and any of the 20 or so short roads you pass on the left running off Ocean Street and Pittwater Road, will take you to the beach and the pounding Pacific Ocean.

Collaroy Beach was named after the 'Collaroy', a coastal paddle steamer that was blown onto the beach on January 20th 1882. The ship stuck firmly in the sand and remained there for over two and a half years before it was refloated on September 19th 1884 and resumed its trading activities.

Narrabeen was the tram terminus on the Manly line between 1913 and 1939 when the line closed. D.H.Lawrence, who travelled on the tram from Manly in 1922, recounted in his novel 'Kangaroo', "The tram took them five or six miles to the terminus. This was the end of everywhere, with new 'stores' – that is fly-blow shops with corrugated iron roofs – and with a tram-shelter, and little house-agents' booths plastered with signs…" The tram shelter is still there at Narrabeen on Pittwater Road, now used as a bus shelter.,

Passing through Collaroy shops then Long Reef Golf Links on the left, as Pittwater Road sweeps round to the right, *Dee Why Lagoon Wildfowl Reserve* can be seen below, while just to the left as you round the corner, is an access road to *Long Reef Beach*. On most days windsurfers can be seen practising wave-jumping just here. As Pittwater Road enters Dee Why, turn left into Dee Why Parade, follow it to the end of *Dee Why Beach*, then turn right to follow Griffin Road up and over the crest of a rise, from the top of which there is a view to Manly and North Head. After descending the hill and crossing the bridge over

Harbord Lagoon, drive straight on into Carrington Parade, and follow it as it passes the southern end of *Curl Curl Beach*. Keep to the left to follow the road at the top of the cliff around McKillop Park, pass *Harbord Beach* below you on the left and join Evans Street.

Now it's just a question of setting your sights for Circular Quay. At the end of Evans Street turn left along Albert Street, through Harbord shops, then turn left at Oliver Street, turn left again at the bottom of Oliver Street at the traffic lights into Pittwater Road, at Manly Golf Links go straight on into Balgowlah Road and take the first right into Kenneth Road. At the first set of traffic lights on Kenneth Road turn left into Condamine Street and now you are virtually home and dry. This is the main highway to Sydney, just follow the signs for the next 12 kilometres to take you over the Spit and Harbour bridges back to the city.

On the way, or on another day, take Awaba Street on the left off Spit Road to Balmoral, the Queen of Sydney Harbour beaches. Balmoral is named after the Royal Family's estate in Scotland, built by Queen Victoria in 1853. The bay is really two beaches, Edwards at the north and Balmoral at the south, separated by a tiny isthmus leading to a little grassy park studded with trees at Rocky Point. The point becomes an island during spring high tides, joined to the promenade at Balmoral by a concrete footbridge.

Another interesting diversion in the area, particularly for the kids, is *Middle Head Fort*.

Middle Head Fort

Middle Head and neighbouring Georges Heights are riddled with a whole network of lookouts, passages, tunnels, stairways and ammunition stores, mostly created in two feverish bursts of activity during the 'Russian Scare' of 1871 and at the start of the Second World War. In the 1860s, Russian warships were taking more than a casual interest in Australian

ports during long distance "training expeditions", and the creation of an effective defence for Sydney during the Second World War was spurred on by the Japanese midget sub attack on Sydney Harbour.

To get to the old fortifications, turn left on Military Road at Spit Junction, then left on Middle Head Road, and park at the car park near the corner of Chowder Bay Road and Middle Head Road. Walk through Middle Head Oval and behind the army barracks, cross a patch of rough ground to a well preserved weatherboard cottage, then take the straight track that runs directly onto the headland.

The guns of the fort were never fired in anger, but four men were killed on April 4th, 1891 when a mine accidentally exploded. The National Parks and Wildlife Service organise tours of the fort during school holidays.

A walk on the Wild Side

Tonight if you still have the energy,

grab a cab and go to *Kings Cross.* Kings Cross, or 'The Cross' as it is usually known in Sydney, was called Queen's Cross in 1897 after the Diamond Jubilee of Queen Victoria, then renamed Kings Cross in 1904 after Edward VII. The 'Cross' part of the title comes from the intersection of five roads at Kings Cross at the junction of William Street and Darlinghurst Road.

Kings Cross is certainly the King of vice in Sydney these days, with prostitutes hanging out on the street corners, a number of strip joints lining Darlinghurst Road and a flourishing drug trade on the streets. Although with that said, the Cross is the most lively area in Sydney for night life, boasting some good restaurants and nightclubs, with souvenir and other shops staying open until well into the night.

After a night on the town in Sydney it's nice to see the harbour at first light. Early morning activity on Sydney Harbour photographed from Potts Point near Kings Cross. The Canberra has just come through the heads, while off Bradleys Head a freighter is overtaken by the Manly Ferry on its way to Sydney. Another ferry and a hydrofoil go by in the opposite direction on their way to Manly as two tugs wait to pick up the Canberra when she passes by. The hydrofoils were taken out of service in 1992 and replaced by jetcats, a fast style of catamaran.

THURSDAY

Thursday

Stately buildings and famous Bondi Beach

Journeying by car to the University, then Victoria Barracks, we go through the terraced houses of Paddington, and onto Bondi Beach, before visiting The Gap, Watsons Bay, Vaucluse House and returning to Sydney.

At the end of Circular Quay, turn up Phillip Street, cross Chifley Square into Elizabeth Street and follow it down to the south end of Hyde Park, where, if you've made an early start, you should be able to find a parking spot at one of the parking meters. Make sure that you leave your hotel with a pocketful of $1 coins, Sydney's parking meters have a voracious appetite.

Hyde Park

In the centre of Hyde Park stands the *Sydney War Memorial* and *Pool of Remembrance*. The building of the Memorial was financed by 60,000 pounds collected from a fund opened on April 25, 1916, the first anniversary of the landing of Australian and New Zealand troops at Gallipoli. Following a design competition the memorial was planned and constructed by Sydney architect Bruce Dellit, with the sculptures the work of Raynor Hoff. Hoff, born in Nottingham, England learnt his basic stone working skills in his father's masonry yard before serving in the trenches in France during the Great War and later moving to Australia, where he taught sculpture at Sydney Technical College.

Dellit felt 'the monument… must be purely contemporary in its style' with the sculptures designed to represent the sacrifice of war, and, 'to give an impression, not of the glory of war, but of its tragedy and horror'.

When Hoff completed plaster models of his sculptures for the memorial in 1932, they included two large groups to be placed on the pedestals beneath the east and west windows. One of the groups, titled 'The Crucifixion of Civilisation' included the figure of a nude woman on the cross, prompting an outcry of protest from many church leaders, but admiration from others. The ceremony of laying the foundation stone of the memorial was not attended by the Roman Catholic Archbishop of Sydney, Michael Sheehan, because he claimed the memorial is 'obviously intended only for Protestants' and that the sculpture 'The Crucifixation of Civilisation' is 'gravely offensive to ordinary Christian decency'. His private secretary added 'What we do object to particularly is the figure of the woman on the cross – a perfectly nude woman, which is immoral and revolting in a memorial like that'. Hoff replied 'that no members of the services who had seen the sculptures objected to them. The Vatican contains dozens of representations of figures in the nude, but it is complained that the nude figure of peace is objectionable'. However, when the memorial was completed funds weren't available to cast the controversial sculptures in bronze, and the plaster models were stored for a time and subsequently lost.

Underneath the memorial the basement holds an exhibition of photographs on Australians at War.

Entry is through the door outside the memorial on the west side facing the city.

Since 1958 a ceremonial Guard of Honour has been mounted by troops of the Australian Army outside the memorial on special occasions.

Two minutes walk from the Anzac Memorial at the south east corner of the park is a gun taken from the *Emden* following the battle of the Cocos Islands in 1914. The 105mm gun was forged by the Krupp works at Essen, Germany in 1904. A traversing wheel and the barrel of the gun bear scars sustained during the action. Three Australian sailors and one officer were killed in the engagement.

In Hyde Park north east of the Anzac Memorial is a statue of Captain Cook, erected in 1879, the hundredth anniversary of his death at Owhyhee (Hawaii). Thomas Woolner was commissioned to execute the sculpture, an English sculptor who came to Australia during the gold rush in 1852 but was unsuccessful in his quest for fortune and returned to England in 1854.

Big surf at Bondi Beach (previous pages) with Sydney city in the background.

Hyde Park (right) is a cool oasis in the concrete desert of the city.

Cook discovered the east coast of Australia in 1770 and anchored for a few days in Botany Bay. Cook didn't enter Sydney Harbour, but on leaving Botany Bay and sailing north up the coast mentioned in his journal 'a Bay or Harbour where there appeared to be safe anchor- age which I called Port Jackson (lying), 3 leagues to the northward of Botany Bay'.

Cook's outstretched arm on the statue seems to be gesturing you towards the Australian Museum, directly across the road on College Street.

The Australian Museum

The first museum in Sydney, designed by Colonial Architect Mortimer Lewis in 1846, stood on a site facing William Street on land which during the 1790s had been convict gardens. Part way through construction there was an investigation

Thursday

The Australian Museum (above).

Sydney War Memorial and Pool of Remembrance (top left). Statues and sculptures by Raynor Hoff grace the interior and exterior of the building. One hundred and twenty thousand stars in the white marble dome over the hall represent each Australian man and woman who served in the Great War.

Detail from a bas-relief on the side of the War Memorial (left) captures the toil and tragedy of the First World War.

Seven Days

80

concerning alleged misuse of public funds by Lewis, who resigned, and the museum wasn't opened to the public until 1857. Plaster casts of Greek and Roman antiquities, donated by Sir Charles Nicholson, an early Trustee, were one of the first exhibits.

The present facade of the Australian Museum facing College Street, was Government Architect James Barnet's first major building completed in the colony. Barnet's original proposal was grander even than the British Museum, built 1837-47. It included a lecture theatre, art gallery, sculpture gallery and library as well as a museum. The main entrance facing William Street was to have had a neo-classi-

cal design with a broad flight of steps approaching a columned portico of twelve paired Corinthian columns backed by a large dome. However the only part of Barnet's ambitious scheme to be completed was the present day west wing facing College Street, finished with, as Barnet described it in 1866, '... the tympanum of the pediment... left plain in the hope that at a future day it will be adorned by some emblematic group of sculpture'. However the tympanum has remained bare to this day, and its vacant triangle gazes blankly towards the city. The first floor galleries were supported (and are still supported) by wrought iron tubular

Sydney University (above) was founded in 1852, on the Great Western Highway just outside the city centre. When the University was completed, the land between it and the city was still devoted to cow pastures. The Great Hall at the university is considered one of the top ten examples of architecture in Australia.

Thursday

Central Station Clocktower (above). As imposing a clock tower as you will see anywhere.

The former prison chapel (top right) and the entrance gateway to Darlinghurst Gaol (above right), which are now part of East Sydney Technical College. The gaol walls date from 1824, and the entrance gate to the 1870s.

Construction of the enclosing gaol walls was started by Francis Greenway using convict labour, then the gaol was completed to the design of Mortimer Lewis when Greenway was dismissed as colonial architect.

When the gaol was converted into a technical college early this century, the interior cell walls of the cell blocks were demolished and the windows enlarged, but otherwise the general appearance of the gaol has changed very little. A stroll through the grounds will reveal the prison chapel (turned into a library), the Governor's Residence (now the principal's office), the gaol morgue (a switchroom), the gallows yard (a ladies and gents toilet) and the cell blocks (converted into ceramics, art and fashion studios and a theatre).

Victoria Barracks (top far right) was built by Lieutenant-Colonel George Barney of the Royal Engineers, who had worked in the West Indies designing fortifications and barracks. The barracks is one of the longest buildings in Australia, being about as long as the Queen Mary. Some of the detail work in the building is quite interesting, such as the drains from the roof which run inside the verandah pillars, and the cast-iron air vents in the wall, decorated with the Royal Crown.

The Changing of the Guard ceremony at Victoria Barracks (following page above), follows a guided tour of the barracks. The tour includes a look at Busby's bore, a deep vertical shaft to a tunnel bored through the sandstone for 3.4 kilometres from Lachlan Swamps at the present site of Centennial Park to Hyde Park. The bore, Sydney's first water supply, was started by J. Busby using convict labour, in 1827. Prisoners at the nearby military gaol in the barracks hauled thousands of gallons of water a day up the shaft using a hand windlass.

girders 'the first ever made in the Colony'.

The Museum was opened to the public in 1868, with displays of animals, fish, insects and minerals. Attendance in 1872 was 240,920, nearly half the entire population of New South Wales. A new wing was later added to the museum facing William street, but nothing like Barnet's original proposal and built to an austere modern design.

A free 30 minute orientation tour through the Museum starts on the ground floor at 10.00am, 12 noon and 2.00pm. See the exhibition Mammals in Australia, and ponder the sad fate of those no longer in existence, including the Thylacine (Tasmanian Tiger), once the largest living marsupial carnivore, deliberately hunted to extinction in Tasmania by the mid 1930s because they killed sheep. A vicious looking beast all the same. Other Australian creatures no longer with us include the pig-footed bandicoot and the Toolache wallaby. The skeletons exhibit has a great display of a human skeleton sitting in a lounge room in his armchair with a skeleton of a dog by his side, a skeleton of a cat in the corner about to pounce on the skeleton of a mouse and a skeleton of a bird on its perch in a bird cage.

Lust after the gemstones in the Planet of Minerals. Experience the Dreamtime of the extinguishing aboriginal culture in the Aboriginal Australia exhibit, where it's not hard to feel a twinge of sadness at the tragedy of a dispossessed people who in 200 years have abruptly woken up to the realities of modern civilisation while the rest of the Western world has had 20,000 years to get used to the idea. However life goes on, and none of us feel guilty enough to want to return to our countries of origin because of it. See Eric the opalised pilasaur from Coober Pedy, South Australia in the More than Dinosaurs exhibit. Pilosaurs are an extinct marine reptile that lived in the shallow seas covering inland Central Australia 110-120 million years ago. Aussie fossils

Thursday

on display include an example of the largest known bird that ever lived in the world, which became extinct about six million years ago. It was even bigger than the famed elephant bird of Madagascar, and its fossilised remains were discovered in the Northern Territory. There's also the fossilised skeleton of a Diprotoden, the largest known marsupial of all time, a beak mouthed creature the size of a rhino which we believe looked like a cross between a wombat and a koala which could have survived until as recently as 10,000 years ago.

A terrific feature on Human Evolution includes the story of the Lake Mungo people from western New South Wales, a modern branch of Homo Sapiens who buried their dead with elaborate rituals 30,000 years ago. Last but not least, make sure to match your wits with the marine invertebrates on the top floor. The Australian Museum also has temporary special exhibitions, and you may be lucky enough to catch one

of the major travelling world exhibitions on display. The museum shop on the ground floor includes one of the best bookshops in Sydney.

Broadway

Continuing on Elizabeth Street turn right under the sandstone railway bridge into Hay Street, turn left into George Street and at Railway Square branch right into *Broadway* following the signpost for Parramatta. Pass an extraordinary example of Victoria Bank architecture on the corner of Regent Street, and Carlton United Breweries, brewers of Fosters Lager on the left. Continue on Broadway to a pedestrian bridge over the road, just past which are some car parking spaces on the left. Some steps near the footbridge lead into the University Grounds.

Sydney University, design by Colonial Architect *Edmund Blacket* and built between 1854-1860, is like a corner of Oxford uprooted and transported to Australia. With its lush green lawns and cool cloisters

it's a haven from the nearby traffic and crowds of the city. Ask if you can go into the stately *Great Hall* adjoining the main quadrangle, with its intricate vaulted wooden roof and beautiful stained glass windows.

Museums

The University is home to two museums, *The Macleay Museum* of Zoology, Anthropology and Photography, on Science Road near the north entrance to the main quadrangle, houses the collection of the Macleay family, donated to the University in 1873. Including specimens gathered by Captain Cook, Charles Darwin and Sir Stamford Raffles, the museum is open from 9.00am to 5.00pm Tuesday to Friday. It isn't very well patronised, so be prepared to search out the caretaker to open the door!

The entrance to the *Nicholson Museum of Antiquities* leads off the south entrance to the main quadrangle. The museum was started in 1860 by Sir Charles Nicholson, with about

100 Greek vases and 400 Egyptian antiquities acquired in Egypt on his way to England in 1856. The collection has been steadily expanded ever since. Opening times are 10.00am to 4.30pm Monday to Friday.

After leaving the University, backtrack along Broadway, drive straight across Railway Square into Pitt Street and turn right at Eddy Avenue past *Central Railway Station.*

Central, Sydney's only mainline railway terminus, was built in 1906 on the site of Devonshire Street Cemetery, once the city's main burial ground.

Before construction could start the coffins were dug up and re-interred at Botany Cemetery. The grand clock tower on the north west corner of Central, the tallest clock tower in Sydney, was added some time after the rest of the station was completed.

Turn left into Elizabeth Street, then follow Wentworth Avenue and Liverpool Street to the forbidding sandstone walls of East Sydney

Technical College on Forbes Street. The walls were not built to keep the students in, but to stop the prisoners from getting out who were inmates of Darlinghurst Gaol, Sydney's prison from 1841 until 1914 when the gaol was converted into a technical college.

Victoria Barracks

Turn left at Taylor Square into Oxford Street and find a place to park near Glenmore Road opposite *Victoria Barracks.* The barracks, an immaculate example of Georgian architecture and one of the best preserved colonial barracks in the world, are open to the public every Thursday at 10.00am, for an interesting free guided tour of the grounds conducted by ex-servicemen. After the tour a changing of the guard takes place accompanied by music from the 2nd Military District Band. The barracks are closed in December and January. Included in the tour is a visit to the army museum in the old military prison of the barracks, where there

Paddington terraces (above, left and far left) were built as working mens' houses in the 1880s and 1890s. Sydney was just a short tram ride away down Oxford Street. Then the suburb declined, commuters moved to more spacious houses further out from the city and by the end of the Second World War, Paddington had turned into a slum. But since the 1960s it has become fashionable again to live in terraces close to the city and people have moved in and restored them.

Thursday

Seven Days

Left page : Bondi Beach (top), Tamarama Bay (centre), and Bronte Beach (bottom). An oceanside path follows the cliff line from the south end of Bondi Beach to Bronte Beach.

Staying on the path for a further six or seven kilometres takes you through Waverley Cemetery and past Clovelly Beach to Coogee Beach (left).

Laing Point (left) with Camp Cove on the left and Watsons Bay on the right. Camp Cove was the first place in the harbour where white settlers stepped ashore. A party of longboats, including Governor Phillip, set up camp there for the night after rowing from Botany Bay, while some aborigines shouted from the high ground close to the cove 'Wara Wara' (go away). Phillip later wrote to England 'The natives are far more numerous than they were supposed to be'.

The cliffs that form the boundary of the eastern suburbs of Sydney (left). The Signal Station (foreground) and Macquarie Lighthouse (background) stand next to Old South Head Road.

Following pages : The Gap, Watsons Bay, with Sydney Harbour in the background.

Thursday

are displays of arms, uniforms and memorabilia from the various campaigns the Australian Army has been involved in over the years.

Victoria Barracks was constructed between 1841 and 1848 by *Lieutenant Colonel George Barney* of the Royal Engineers, with the help of 150 French-Canadian convicts transported to Australia following rebellions in Canada in 1837-38, and non-convict stonemasons and carpenters. Built to accommodate a British Regiment of 800 soldiers and their families, the barracks was the base of British garrison regiments in Sydney until the first New South Wales Artillery and Infantry

South Head (right) and H.M.A.S. Watson Naval Reserve. Lady Bay nudist beach is on the right.

The red and white striped Hornby Lighthouse (right page top) on South Head, was constructed after the tragedy of the Dunbar. Sydney Harbour and the city are in the background.

units were raised in 1870. Although the sandstone for the walls was quarried in Sydney, the slate on the roof of the barracks, the iron columns of the verandahs, the windows, many interior fittings and most of the cedar joinery work was brought out from England.

Paddington

Returning to the car, head up Glenmore Road for a short detour around the streets of *Paddington* to see the terraced houses. The whole district has been classified by the National Trust as an example of architecture worthy of preservation. Most of the terraces were built by

working-class men when the area was sub-divided and sold off for building in the 1880s and 1890s. Because the lots were bought and built on by individuals rather than developers, there's a tremendous variety of style in the houses, particularly in their white facades decorated in cast iron lace-work.

Follow Glenmore Road into Gurner Street and turn right up Cascade Street, that follows the line of old Glenmore Falls, used as a source of water for a gin distillery operating in the area early last century. Pass through Paddington Street and Jersey Road to rejoin Oxford Street.

St Peter's Church of England at Watsons Bay (bottom left).

Doyle's Restaurant on the beach at Watsons Bay (bottom right), Australia's most famous seafood restaurant, has been owned and operated by the same family for over 100 years.

Head west on Oxford Street following the signs for Bondi. At Bondi Road a long straight hill about five kilometres long runs down to Campbell Parade and *Bondi Beach*. In the old days the trams used to thunder down this hill at great speed, sometimes not even stopping for passengers and giving rise to the expression 'shot through like a Bondi tram'.

Bondi Beach

Along with Waikiki, Brighton, St. Tropez and Malibu; Bondi – pronounced Bon-Dye – ranks among the most famous beaches in the world. Indeed the sea at Bondi is held with the same sort of reverence by many

a Sydney surfer as the Ganges is by a Hindu. The beach owes its call to fame by being the closest ocean beach to Sydney, paying a price in summer by attracting crowds of over 25,000 people. It boasts one of Australia's oldest Life Saving Clubs, founded in 1906. If you go for a ritual swim, bathe between the red and yellow flags where the area is patrolled by lifesavers. If walking is more your line, an oceanside track follows the Pacific Ocean for several kilometres from the south end of Bondi Beach to Tamarama, Bronte and Coogee beaches.

Drive around Bondi Beach on Campbell Parade to Military Road

and follow it for four kilometres to Old South Head Road. After about a further kilometre the road passes the majestic, tall, brilliant white *Macquarie Lighthouse*. The lighthouse itself is not open to the public, but visitors are welcome to walk in the grounds. Convict architect *Francis Greenway* received a ticket of leave after designing the original lighthouse, which stood on the site from 1816 to 1881.

A short distance further on New South Head Road you pass the hexagonal sided tower of the *Signal Station*, built in the 1840s. The station has been continually manned since January 1790, when Governor

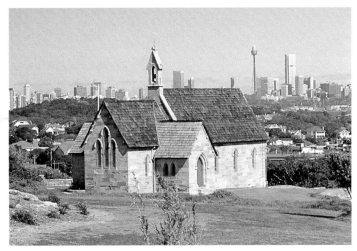

Aerial view of Rushcutters Bay and Sydney (right) photographed from over Darling Point.

Sydney's most popular walking track (below) follows the coast from Bondi to Coogee.

Phillip, anxious that the expected Second Fleet might miss the entrance to Sydney Harbour, sent a party of men to the Head to erect a signal flagstaff and keep a fire burning at night. Shipping movements are logged from the tower to this day. In 1858 the first telegraph line in Sydney ran from the Royal Exchange building in Bridge Street to the Signal Station.

Watsons Bay

Where Old South Head Road curves left to begin the descent to Watsons Bay, the green grass of The Gap Park marks one of Sydney's more morbid tourist attractions. The 50 metre high cliffs are Sydney's tradi-tional location for suicides. Sydney's worst single tragedy occurred here on the night of August 20, 1857, when the migrant ship *Dunbar* was blown onto the rocks below The Gap and all but one of the 122 on board were drowned. Its anchor, recovered in 1907, can be seen mounted in concrete in the park. The sole survivor, *Able Seaman James Johnson,* clung to a rock ledge for 36 hours after the ship went down before he was spotted and thrown a rope. Johnson went on to become lighthouse keeper at Nobbys Head at the entrance to Newcastle Harbour north of Sydney.

Near the road the tiny *St Peters Church of England* designed by Edmund Blacket and completed in 1864, was built on the hill with the hope it would be the first building to greet the eyes of passengers arriving in Sydney by ship. According to a brass plaque at the back of the church, the organ, built by Robert and William Grey of London in 1796 was once used by Napoleon on the island of St. Helena.

Drive down to *Watsons Bay* and park near Military Road next to Robertson Park. Watsons Bay is named after *Robert Watson,* former Quarter Master of the Sirius, the flagship of the First Fleet. After being posted to the Signal Station in 1791, then working as Harbour Master controlling the pilot boats at

Watsons Bay, Watson was made the first Lighthouse Keeper when the Macquarie Lighthouse started operations in 1816 and maintained the light until he died in 1819. Watsons Bay is still the base for pilot boats operating in the harbour.

Doyle's

If it's around lunchtime, consider visiting *Doyle's Restaurant* on the beach at Watsons Bay, Australia's most famous seafood restaurant, owned and operated by the same family for over 100 years. From the tables there's a view right along the length of Sydney Harbour to the city, nine kilometres away. To miss lunch at Doyle's would be like com-ing to Sydney without seeing the Opera House. Make sure to book though. If you don't make it to Watsons Bay, Doyle's also have seafood restaurants at the Fish Markets and Circular Quay.

Returning to the car, head north and follow the one-way system around Watsons Bay to the car park on Cliff Street near the junction with Victoria Street, leave the car and walk to *Camp Cove*. In 1788, when the First Fleet landed at Botany Bay, the settlers found the area swampy and unsuitable for set-tlement. Governor Phillip set out with three long boats to explore Port Jackson (Sydney Harbour) which Cook had sailed past in the Endeavour in 1770 without stopping to explore. After rounding South Head with his party, Phillip stopped for the night at Camp Cove on January 21 1788, thus making Camp Cove the first place where European people stepped ashore in Sydney.

South Head

From Camp Cove a 40 minute return walk leads to *South Head*. At the north end of the cove walk up the wooden steps to an old road paved with sandstone slabs and follow it to a gun emplacement containing a sizeable cannon on an iron carriage manufactured by W.G. Armstrong & Co. Newcastle on Tyne in 1872. Keep to the path on top of the rocks, past

Thursday

Shark Beach (right) is a misnomer. There has not been a shark attack in Sydney for over 20 years. Anyway, the beach is protected by a safety net just to make sure.

Shark Beach at Nielsen Park (below). The red roof of Greycliffe House, completed in 1852, can be seen in the trees to the right of the beach. Macquarie Lighthouse is in the distance.

Stately Vaucluse House (bottom).

Milk Beach and Strickland House (right page) are accessible via a walking track through the Hermitage Foreshore Reserve. The reserve is on Rose Bay between the bottom of Bayview Hill Road and Nielsen Park.

The brilliant white Macquarie Lighthouse (far right) looks like an ad for washing powder.

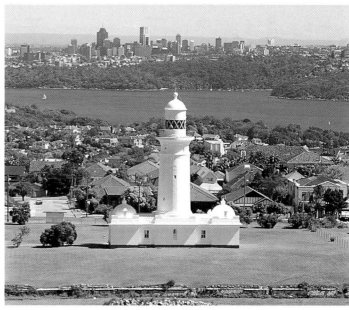

Lady Bay, one of Sydney's two official nudist beaches, to reach South Head after a further 10 minutes walk. At the tip of the Head stands the red and white striped *Hornby Lighthouse,* completed in 1858 after the tragedy of the Dunbar. The lighthouse was named after Sir Phipps Hornby, Commander in Chief of the British Pacific Fleet. Scattered about the head are old fortifications dating from the 1870s to the Second World War.

Vaucluse House

Backtrack to the car and take Hopetoun Avenue out of Watsons Bay. Turn right down Fitzwilliam Road past Parsley Bay into Wentworth Road and after a few hundred metres, turn left up the drive and into the car park in the grounds of *Vaucluse House.*

Vaucluse House received its name from the "Gentleman Convict", Sir Henry Brown Hayes, who is thought to have named if after Fontaine-de-Vaucluse in France, where an underground stream emerges into a steep sided valley in a setting not dissimilar to that of Vaucluse in Sydney. Hayes, an Irish Baronet, was transported for abducting a Quaker heiress and forcing her to marry him. He bought Vaucluse and 100 surrounding acres for 100 pounds in 1803 and built a stone cottage there. Being frightened by snakes, Hayes imported barrels full of Irish soil which was dug into a trench around his house by a gang of convicts. The walls of Hayes' 1803 house comprise the walls of the living room in the present home, making Vaucluse House, in part at least, the oldest house in Sydney.

These days Vaucluse House is substantially the same as it was in about 1840, when it was rebuilt to suit the taste of *William Charles Wentworth* who bought the house in 1827 from Captain John Piper. W.C.Wentworth was fathered from a union between D'Arcy Wentworth, an Assistant Surgeon travelling out to Australia with the Second Fleet and Catherine Crawley, a convict woman transported for stealing clothes, travelling on the same ship. William Charles went on to become one of the 'greats' of Sydney's early colonial days as an explorer, author, barrister and statesman. Read all about this remarkable man in the museum at the house.

From Vaucluse House it's a short walk or drive along Wentworth Road and Greycliffe Avenue to a sheltered harbour swimming beach at *Nielsen Park.* Nearby *Greycliffe House,* completed in 1852, was once part of the Wentworth estate.

A Sydney Harbour ferry, the 'Greycliffe', was involved in Sydney's worst ferry disaster. Travelling from Circular Quay to Watsons Bay at 4.15pm on November 3, 1927, the Greycliffe was sliced in two by the liner 'Tahiti'. Forty two people were drowned including seven children on their way home from school.

Returning to the car, join Vaucluse Road passing the *Convent of the Sacred Heart* (1884) looming over the tranquil waters of Rose Bay like Colditz Castle, and turn right onto New South Head Road, the main road back to Sydney.

Tonight, consider trying the Summit Restaurant on top of Australia Square, off George Street. On the 47th level, the restaurant is the largest tower-top revolving restaurant in the world and takes an hour and three quarters to revolve the full circle. A pianist plays Monday to Saturday and there is a small dance floor. Complimentary night parking is available in the basement off George Street. The cuisine is international with the emphasis on fresh local seafood or there is a choice of buffet luncheon or dinner.

FRIDAY

Friday

In the steps of the First Fleeters

Today's itinerary includes a guided tour of the Opera House and a stroll through the historic Rocks area of Sydney.

———————————————

From *Circular Quay,* follow the paved walkway around the cove to Circular Quay East. If the passers-by are looking at the ground it's not because they're gloomy or have lost two bob, but because they're looking at the quotes by Australian and overseas authors on the brass plaques of the "Writers Walk". Take two minutes to glance at some of them as the aboriginal buskers play the didgeridoo.

Previous pages : Sydney Opera House and the Bennelong Restaurant floodlit at dusk. Two days after the First Fleet landed, some cattle and horses were put ashore on a small island just off the eastern tip of Sydney Cove. A local aborigine, 'Bennelong', that Governor Phillip had captured to 'civilise' was housed on Cattle Island in a brick hut. In 1817 Governor

Macquarie built a fort on the island and linked it to the shore by a drawbridge. In 1902 the fort was demolished to make way for a red-brick mock-gothic battlemented tram depot, which in turn came down in 1958 to make way for the Opera House. The land on which the Opera House stands has been known as Bennelong Point ever since Bennelong lived there.

Government House (below left) residence of the Governor of New South Wales, the Queen's representative in New South Wales. Members of the Royal Family often stay there while visiting Australia. The Tudor style structure with crenellations, tall chimneys and small towers was designed by London architect Edward *Blore, special architect to William IV and then to Queen Victoria. The house was constructed 1837-45.*

The 1,056,000 tiles on the Opera House, (sources vary as to the precise number), cover an area of 4 acres, and are bonded to 4,228 chevron shaped tile panels or 'lids' which were manufactured on the ground then lifted into place and slotted onto the surface of the shells. Eschewing conventional tiles "they give you an impression of paint", the architect specified two special types of tiles for the Opera House roof. A glossy off-white tile with a rippled surface to cut down on glare and a cream coloured tile with a smooth matt surface. The tiles were arranged in subtle patterns, "the fine lines defining the form of the curve like the seams in a billowing sail" (Utzon).

Friday

Mark Twain, who came to Australia in 1895, wrote –

'Australian history is almost always picturesque, indeed it is so curious and strange, that it is itself the chiefest novelty the country has to offer. It does not read like history, but like the most beautiful lies. It is full of surprises, and adventures, and incongruities, and incredibilities, but they are all true, they all happened'.

And Arthur Conan Doyle who came here in 1920-21 –

'We all devoted ourselves to surf-bathing, spending a good deal of our day in the water as is the custom of the place'.

Anthony Trollope, who visited in 1871 -

'The idea that Englishmen… are made of paste, whereas the Australian, native or thoroughly acclimatized, is steel all through, I found to be universal'.

Dorothea Mackellar, wrote in "My Country" in 1911 when she was 19 –

'I love a sunburnt country,
A land of sweeping plains,
Of ragged mountain ranges,
Of droughts and flooding rains,
I love her far horizons,
I love her jewel-sea,
Her beauty and her terror –
The wide brown land for me!'.

D.H. Lawrence, who came to Sydney and New South Wales in 1922, wrote in a letter –

'Australia… (is) like a Sleeping Princess on whom the dust of ages has settled. Wonder if she'll ever get up'.

Banjo Paterson wrote in 1902 –

'It's grand to be an unemployed
And lie in the Domain,
And wake up every second day –
And go to sleep again.'.

Charles Darwin wrote from Australia in 1836 –

'This is really a wonderful Colony; ancient Rome, in her Imperial grandeur, would not have been ashamed of such an offspring'.

And Neville Shute wrote in 1950 in "A Town Like Alice" –

'"It's a funny thing", Jean said.

"You go to a new country, and you expect everything to be different, and then you find there's such a lot that stays the same".'

At the south east corner of Circular Quay East at the rear of 71 Macquarie Street next to the point where the Circular Quay Railway dives underground, is *Coca-Cola-Quayside,* a museum about Coca-Cola through the ages, particularly the Australian bottling operation run by Coca-Cola Amatil whose offices are located above.

Continue north along Circular Quay East for a short distance, then ascend *Moore Stairs* (1868) on the right to Macquarie Street. Cross Macquarie Street to enter the park opposite and taking the centre path go through the gates (open 8.00am to sunset) outside Government House, turn left and follow the road that skirts the grounds of Government House before entering the *Royal Botanic Gardens.* The grassy slope just here is a good location to take photos of the *Opera House.* Walk down the path, through the entrance gate to the Botanic Gardens and across the forecourt to the Opera House.

Sydney Opera House

The story of the *Opera House* is an opera in itself. The English composer *Eugene Goossens,* a direct descendant of Captain Cook, was appointed Conductor of the Sydney Symphony Orchestra in 1947. Goossens persuaded the government of the day that Sydney should have its own Opera Theatre and that it should be built on Bennelong Point opposite the Harbour Bridge. In March 1956, the year following the announcement by the Government of *Bennelong Point* as the site for an Opera House, Goossens' luggage was searched by customs at the airport when he was returning from an overseas trip, and found to contain a quantity of pornographic photos, films and books. Goossens was tried and found guilty of importing indecent material, he resigned as conductor and left Australia that May.

An international design competition for the Opera House, commissioned by the N.S.W. Government in 1957, with a first prize of £5,000, received 233 entries and was won by the unanimous choice of the four judges, by 38 year old Danish architect *Jorn Utzon.* A team of quantity surveyors examined the top 10 designs from the competition, and worked out that Utzon's plan would cost about $7 million to build, the cheapest they thought, of the 10 they looked at. It was decided that the Opera House would take three years to complete.

To finance the project, a public lottery "The Opera House Lottery" was started. Tragedy struck when following the publicity surrounding the awarding of one of the first prizes of £100,000, the winner's son, eight year old Graeme Thorne, was kidnapped, held to ransom, then murdered after the ransom was paid.

Construction of the Opera House proceeded slowly, largely due to design and construction difficulties associated with the unique architecture of the project. In February 1966, with construction still proceeding on the Opera House shells, Utzon resigned following disagreements with the Country Party Minister Davis Hughes; Minister for Public Works in the new Liberal-Country Party Coalition Government. Pressured for completed working drawings of the interiors, with arguments raging over fees and the structural feasibility of the ceiling of one of the theatres, Utzon wrote in his letter of resignation '… there has been no collaboration on the most vital items of the job in the last many months from your department's side'. Talking of "malice in Blunderland" and later saying "I do not care if they pull the Opera House down", Utzon asked that his name should no longer be associated with the Opera House.

Utzon's design for the interior of the Opera House was shelved (the drawings were not complete), and the design of the interior and the completion of the project was overseen by a team of four Australian architects, with Peter Hall as design architect.

By the time the Opera House was officially opened by the Queen on Saturday October 10, 1973, fifteen years after construction had started, the final cost of the project had increased to $S102 million. Jorn Utzon declined his invitation to attend the opening, and to date has never returned to Australia to see his completed masterpiece.

The years following the completion of the Opera House have proved its success, not only as a design exercise, but as a performance venue. The acoustics of the Concert Hall are rated among the top three theatres in the world, while the complex of five theatres at the Opera House is one of the busiest performing arts centres in the world, with an average of over 2,900 events held every year, from conventions to grand opera.

Opera House Tours

Guided tours of the Opera House leave approximately every half an hour, seven days a week, from the lower concourse walkway on the south-west side of the Opera House.

A tour fee is charged. Privately conducted tours of the Opera House are available and backstage tours on Sundays.

Seats for theatres can be booked by phoning the Sydney Opera House Box Office. Alternatively, if you wish to call at the box office itself, it is in the Opera House foyer, accessible from the staircase leading up from the vehicle concourse, or through the exterior foyer doors off the first landing of the podium reached after a climb up the monumental staircase.

From the Opera House, return to Circular Quay, walk past the ferry wharves and turn right onto Circular Quay West to reach *Cadman's Cottage*, near the *Overseas Passenger Terminal*. An interesting alternative route to Cadman's Cottage would be to ascend *Tarpeian Steps* in front of the Opera House forecourt, walk through the park to Macquarie Street, ascend a flight of stairs up to the Cahill Expressway footpath, and with an elevated view of Circular Quay follow the expressway to the stairs at Cumberland Street and wend your way through The Rocks to Cadman's Cottage.

The Tarpeian Steps received their name because the rock at the point that they are cut from was jestingly referred to as the "Tarpeian Rock" by the First Fleet soldiers after the rock in ancient Rome from which traitors were thrown to their death. The "Tarpeian Way" next to the paling fence in the park at the top of the steps, was the route the convicts used after arriving in Sydney by ship to get to Hyde Park Barracks.

From the Cahill Expressway footpath there is a good view of the Circular Quay area. On the left, the Overseas Passenger Terminal was the point where hundreds of thousands of European migrants arriving in Australia disembarked in the 1950s and 1960s. In the 1950s when planning was going ahead for a new Passenger Terminal, the New South Wales Minister for Public Works wanted to build it on the site of the tram depot at Bennelong Point, but Goosens persuaded Premier Cahill that the Opera House should go at Bennelong Point and the Passenger Terminal should remain on the west side of the cove.

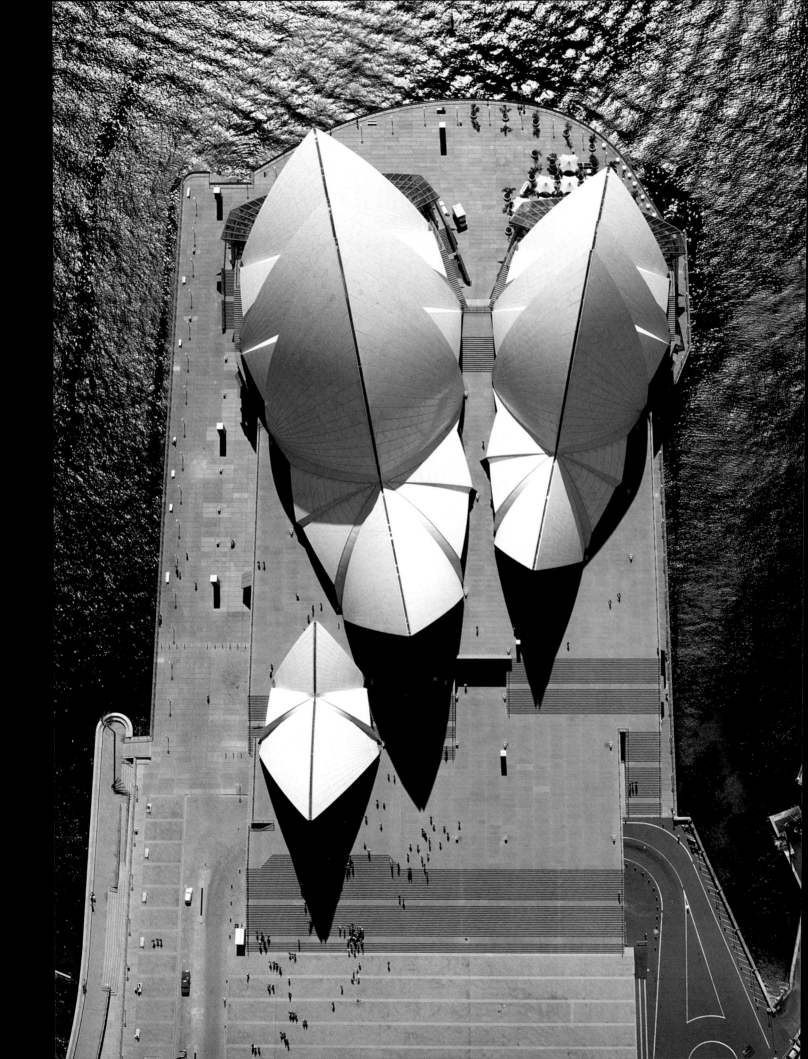

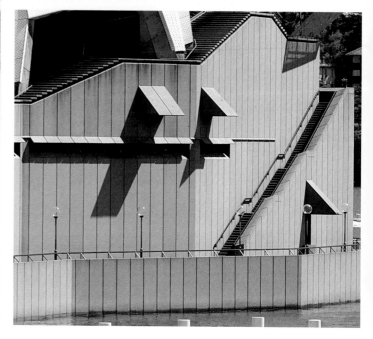

Previous two pages : Details of the base or 'podium' of the Opera House (left page) a formidable sculpture in itself. The podium cladding and paving, finished with a surface of ground pink granite chips, was intended by Utzon "to give the rock-like character desired for the base, as a contrast and anchor to the soaring roofs".

Right page, top. "It gives the impression of a wonderful piece of sculpture, deliberately placed to be seen from all points of view", wrote Denis Winston, Professor of Town Planning at Sydney University, on seeing the competition winning design for the first time in January 1957.

Below. The monumental stairs of the podium conceal a vehicle concourse.

The Rocks and the area around Circular Quay, was the first area of white settlement in Australia. When the 1,030 people of the First Fleet, including 500 male, 200 female convicts and 13 children, landed in January 1788, they cleared the bush, and built a bakery, a store, a hospital, mens and womens camps and huts for the soldiers from trees, bark and branches of local mimosa or 'wattle' as they called it after 'wattle and daub'.

The building of Circular Quay itself was supervised by Colonel George Barney, designer of Victoria Barracks. In a work that took seven years, involved the labour of thousands of convicts and the quarrying of tens of thousands of tons of rock from harbour headlands, islands and *Argyle Cut* , Barney reclaimed five hectares at the estuary of the Tank Stream, dredged Sydney Cove using the 'Hercules' a locally built steam dredge and built sea walls to form the horse-shoe shaped 'Semi-Circular Quay'.

The Rocks

Cadman's Cottage, unused and derelict in 1972, has been restored to resemble its original condition by the National Parks and Wildlife Service, who have an information centre inside. The cottage, the oldest dwelling in Sydney, was built in 1816 for John Cadman, transported

to Australia in 1798 for stealing a horse. Cadman was made Government Coxswain by Macquarie, received a conditional pardon, and was later promoted to 'Superintendent of Government Boats', a post he held from 1827 to 1846, when he retired aged 88.

Walk up the steps next to Cadman's Cottage into George Street, and turn right to the *Sydney Visitors Centre* in the old Sailors' Home. The centre is a mine of information on Sydney and has free maps and information booklets on the city. The *Sydney Cove Authority* helps to run the *Centre*. The *Authority* was set up by an Act of Parliament in 1968 'To develop Sydney Cove as the

Gateway to Sydney, keeping in mind the past, present and the future.' Over the years the authority has completed a lot of useful work in The Rocks restoring old buildings.

The Sailors' Home was built by a charitable society to provide low cost accommodation for the crews of sailing ships. In the early nineteenth century under a practice known as 'crimping' sailors arriving in port were frequently met by tricksters known as 'crimps' posing as masters of registered boarding houses, who would take the sailor to a brothel or bar and get him drunk when an accomplice would rob him of his savings. The crimp would then 'sell' the indebted sailor to another ship's cap-

The north facing foyers of the Opera Theatre and Concert Hall, enclosed by glass walls (top left), offer panoramic views of Sydney Harbour from inside (above).

The west glass walls of the interior of the south foyer of the Concert Hall (above left).

Following page. Top left, the stairs and entrance canopy of the Opera Theatre south foyer, and looking east from the foyer itself (top right). The Concert Hall interior (below).

Friday

Previous page : The interior of the Bennelong Restaurant (top left), and the exterior of the south foyer of the Concert Hall (top right).

Stairs leading from the south to the north Concert Hall foyer (centre left), and descending to the bar area (centre right).

The Concert Hall bar area (bottom).

The "Oriana" on Circular Quay (above). Captain Cook Cruises boat is on the right.

tain, any remaining wages the sailor received went in repaying the new captain and the sailor returned home broke. The home was built to provide the sailor with a clean, decent bed during his stay in the Port of Sydney, though if he preferred an unclean, indecent bed he could just keep walking further up the hill!

A large 'Romanesque Revival' style building was designed in 1860 for the home, but due to lack of funds only the north wing was completed in 1864. Not long after the

home opened in 1868, its President, Sir William Manning, intervened to save the life of Queen Victoria's son Prince Alfred who was shot and wounded by an Irish fanatic during a picnic at Clontarf Reserve on the harbour. A donation of £500 was made by the Prince to the home as a token of gratitude.

Continue on George Street and turn left into Playfair Street. The sandstone *Union Bond Stores* (1841), on the corner, containing a branch of the Westpac Bank with a banking

Clockwise from top left : Victorian buildings line the west side of George Street in The Rocks, Cadman's Cottage is the oldest dwelling in the City of Sydney, The Sydney Visitors Centre is in the old Sailors' Home and a branch of Westpac Bank and a banking museum now occupy the Union Bond Stores on George Street.

museum upstairs, was designed by Ashley Alexander, designer of Dartmoor Prison in England.

Walk the length of Playfair Street and turn right into Argyle Street. A short distance up Argyle Street you pass the entrance to the cobbled courtyard of the *Argyle Stores*. The cobblestones were brought out from England as ballast in the hulls of sailing ships.

One time owner of Argyle Stores, Mary Reibey, transported to Australia as a 13 year old girl, was the most influential businesswoman and merchant in Sydney during the early part of last century. Among her many achievements she worked

in the setting up of the Bank of N.S.W. in 1815 (now Westpac Bank). A letter Mary Reibey wrote home to her aunt on October 8, 1792, the day after she arrived on a convict transport in Sydney, is the earliest surviving letter written by an Australian convict. Her picture appears on the Australian $20 note.

As you continue west on Argyle Street, walk through *Argyle Cut*. The Cut was started in 1843 by convict chain gangs, working by hand to cut rock for the seawalls and the infill at Circular Quay and was completed in 1859 by free labour using blasting. The stone Princes Street Bridge over the cut and the entire length of Princes Street with its houses was

demolished when the Harbour Bridge approaches were built in the 1920s.

Emerge from Argyle Cut to *Argyle Place*, Sydney's only village green, lined by a variety of Georgian and Victorian cottages and terraces, erected between 1840 and 1880. Argyle Place was named in 1810 by Governor Macquarie after his home county in Scotland.

At the east end of Argyle Place near Argyle Cut, Holy Trinity Church known as the *'Garrison Church'*, was used by soldiers of Dawes Point Battery. The first military church in Australia with a foundation stone laid in 1840, it was built from stone quarried by convicts at Argyle Cut. The Garrison

Church was enlarged to a design by Edmund Blacket, completed 1878. A spire included in Blacket's design was never completed. The church is much roomier inside than it appears from the exterior and can seat 600. The east window of the church is considered the finest example of stained glass in Sydney.

Coming out of the church, cross Argyle Street, go up the steps on the left and follow Watson Road and Upper Fort Street to Observatory Hill.

The Observatory and Astronomer's Residence stand on the site of Fort Phillip Citadel, a hexagonal redoubt with sides 100 feet long started in 1804 by Governor King to be used as a last line of defence by the

Government if there was an insurrection by political prisoners. However, the fort was never used and it didn't save Governor Bligh who was overthrown by his own military in 1808. The fort was demolished in the 1840s except for two of the walls which form part of the enclosure of the Sydney Observatory.

The telescopes in the Observatory were used for astronomical research from 1858 to 1982 when the Observatory closed. The building now houses a museum. A time ball on the weather vane on the tower of the Observatory dropped daily at 1.00pm as a signal for a cannon to be fired from Dawes Point and then Fort Denison between 1858 and 1942. The practice was stopped that year following the Japanese midget submarine attack on Sydney Harbour, as it was feared the noise might alarm Sydney residents.

Firing of the gun resumed in 1986, and the dropping of the time ball (now on the sound of the gun) in 1987, though the dropping of the ball is subject to availability of staff and mechanical malfunctions.

In front of the Observatory near a bandstand, a memorial lists the names of men from the units of volunteers from N.S.W., who were killed in the Boer War. A rusting Krupp artillery piece in front of the memorial, captured during the war, was forged in Essen in 1895.

Argyle Stores in The Rocks (above far left).

The convict on the three sided "First Impressions" sculpture (above left).

The Argyle Cut (above) was partly quarried by convicts.

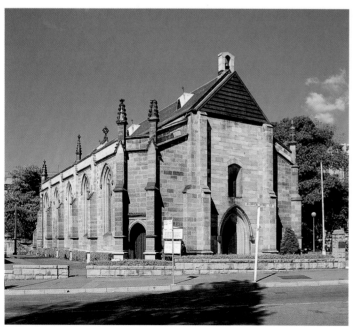

114

Houses on Argyle Place (above left) date from the 1840s to the late Victorian era.

The Garrison Church (left and far left) was originally built for the soldiers of Dawes Point Battery.

Lower Fort Street and the Harbour Bridge from Observatory Hill (above).

Walk south from the Observatory, skirting the cutting of the Cahill Expressway, to the *National Trust Centre;* since 1975 the headquarters of the N.S.W. Branch of the Australian National Trust. The Trust offices are located in a building built in 1815 as a Military Hospital by Governor Macquarie, designed by his young aide-de-camp, Lieutenant John Watts. Originally constructed with double-storeyed verandahs similar to the Mint Museum, the present neo-classical facade was added by colonial architect Mortimer Lewis in 1871. When George Street Barracks moved to Victoria Barracks in 1848, the building was used for Fort Street School

from 1848 to 1974. Behind the main building, the *S.H. Ervin Gallery of Australian Art and Architecture* is housed in an old ward added to the military hospital in 1841.

Backtracking the same way you came towards the Observatory, descend *Agar Steps* to Kent Street, turn right and walk to Argyle Place. Enter the Lord Nelson Hotel on the corner of Kent Street and Argyle Place.

The Lord Nelson Hotel

The white sandstone Lord Nelson Hotel carries the honour of being Sydney's oldest hotel. The first landlord was an ex-convict plasterer, William Wells, who erected the

The Waterfront Restaurant in Campbell's Storehouse at Campbell's Cove (below). The first landlord of the Lord Nelson Hotel (bottom) was an ex-convict plasterer, William Wells. Wells erected the building in 1834 as his residence, using sandstone blocks quarried from the base of Observatory Hill, then in 1841 converted it into the Lord Nelson Hotel.

Observatory Hill (right). The wall of the Observatory (centre of picture) part of the wall of the uncompleted Fort Phillip Citadel, is possibly the oldest European man-made structure existing in Sydney, dating to 1806.

building as his home in 1834 using sandstone blocks quarried from the base of Observatory Hill. In 1838 Wells bought a pub across the road on the north east corner of Kent Street and Argyle Street called The Sailor's Return which he renamed The Quarrymen's Arms. In 1841 he sold that pub and applied for a liquor licence for his home which he then called The Lord Nelson. A pub over the road called The Napoleon ran in competition to the Lord Nelson for a time in the nineteenth century.

These days the Lord Nelson is advertised as 'The pub that restored Nelson's eyesight.' The pub brews its own beers in-house, offering a choice of Trafalgar Pale Ale, Victory Bitter, Quayle Ale or Old Admiral, 6.7% proof brewed in 'traditional dogbolter style - to be taken with great respect.' Unfortunately the Nelson's Blood Stout is no longer available. Various mementoes of the Battle of Trafalgar decorate the walls, including an original copy of the front page of *The Times* newspaper announcing the successful outcome of the battle. According to the cutting, just before engaging the enemy Nelson had said, 'Now they cannot escape us; I think we shall at least make sure of twenty of them. I shall probably lose a leg but that would be purchasing victory cheaply.' Taken below decks

on being mortally wounded, Nelson turned to Captain Hardy and said "'I know I am dying, I could have wished to survive to breathe my last upon British ground, but the will of God be done." A few moments later he expired.'

A brasserie on the 1st floor of the hotel offers 'innovative Australian delights.' Elegant guest rooms on the top floor are decorated and furnished 'to capture the atmosphere of the colonial era.'

Pass the Colonial House Museum at 53 Lower Fort Street (open 10.00am to 5.00pm daily), walk right to the end of Lower Fort Street and onto the grass of Dawes Point

Park beneath the Harbour Bridge approach. Lieutenant William Dawes of the First Fleet constructed a gun battery on the point in 1788 using six naval cannon from the *Sirius*. Dawes, a scientist, had been sent to the colony by the Astronomer Royal to observe Maskelyn's Comet, due to appear in the southern skies late in 1788. A telescope Dawes set up for astronomical observations came to more practical use when it was used to watch signals from the flag station near South Head.

Dawes Battery was enlarged to include five mortars, thirteen 42 pounders, a magazine, soldiers'

quarters and a residence for the C.O. These structures were demolished when the bridge was built, and all that remains today are five cannons cast in 1843 and 1844 resting peacefully on carriages on the grassy slope of the park overlooking the harbour and Opera House.

Archaeologists working on the site in 1995 speculated on the origin of a 2,000 year old Roman silver coin discovered in the battery cess-pit. Did it belong to a soldier who was admiring his coin collection on the john when he dropped one, or was it inadvertently swallowed with the Christmas pudding and passed through the cistern.

Friday

If the cannon Dawes Point Battery (above left) were to fire today, they'd blast a hole in the side of Sydney Opera House on the opposite side of Sydney Cove.

The replica of 'The Bounty' approaching Campbell's Cove (above right).

The Opera House from Dawes Point Park (left).

Detail from a base-relief above the entrance of the Museum of Contemporary Art (right).

The QE2 moored at Sydney Cove Passenger Terminal (right page).

Continue on Hickson Road, forking left onto Circular Quay West to *Campbell's Storehouse*. Robert Campbell built the first private wharf in the colony and ran a prosperous merchant's business from his stores on the waterfront. Campbell's wharf was better built than those provided by the colony's administrators. An officer from

HMS Glatton, who had to strengthen the Government Hospital wharf to unload some guns in 1806, declared 'The only good landing place that had respectable appearance has been erected by a Mr Robert Campbell'. Two restaurants and a wine bar have been tastefully incorporated to blend in with the fabric of the old stores.

That's the end of today's tour. If you have covered even half the ground no doubt you will be worn out and thoroughly deserve a pep-up in the evening by making your way to the Inter-Continental Hotel on the corner of Macquarie and Bridge Streets. From the Cocktail Lounge in the Top of the Treasury Bar on the 31st level, open every night, you can enjoy spectacular views of the Botanical Gardens, Circular Quay, the Opera House and Government House to the accompaniment of a local jazz band.

Friday

SATURDAY

Saturday

Darling Harbour and the City's best view

Start the day at Sydney's Chinatown; see if you can resist the enticing aromas wafting through the doors of the many restaurants. After seeing the Chinese Gardens, Festival Markets and museums at Darling Harbour, catch a ride on the monorail to the ritzy shopping centre of Sydney, taking in the Queen Victoria Building and Centrepoint on the way. Then cross Hyde Park and the Domain to the Art Gallery of N.S.W. Finish the afternoon with a visit to Fort Denison on Sydney Harbour, or with a Captain Cook Cruise on the Harbour.

Hail a cab to *Dixon Street* in the centre of Sydney's *Chinatown*. Many of the restaurants offer a Chinese breakfast if you've missed your own. One of the best is available from the *Shark's Fin* restaurant on the third level of Market City above *Paddy's Market*. Not only does the *Shark's Fin* offer a very reasonably priced Yum Cha (Chinese breakfast) it is also the biggest restaurant in Australia, seating 800. Nearby, on the corner of Hay Street and Harbour Street, the *Sydney Entertainment Centre*, the largest indoor auditorium in Australia, opened in 1983 and seating up to 12,500, is a venue for concerts, ice skating events, indoor tennis tournaments and so on. To find out who's in town and to make bookings go to the booking office in the Centre.

Directly south of the *Entertainment Centre* is *Paddy's Market*, where if it is a Friday, Saturday or Sunday you may be tempted to pick up a bargain at one of the stalls. Outside the Market runs the *Sydney Light Rail*. From Haymarket Station at Paddy's you can take the train to *Central Station* in one direction, or to the *Exhibition Centre, Convention Centre, Casino* and *Fish Markets* in the other.

Head to Little Pier Street north of the *Entertainment Centre*. On your right is the historic *Pump House* which formerly provided hydraulic pressure to operate lifts in the city. The house was built for the Sydney Suburban Hydraulic Power Co., established 1889, which laid a grid of hydraulic pipes through the city and The Rocks for businesses to purchase hydraulic power for a variety of uses including driving machinery. The Pump House was still providing hydraulic power until 1975. The building now accommodates the refurbished Tavern and Boutique Brewery. Here you can see beer being brewed 'on site', though it's probably a little too early to taste the first drop!

The Powerhouse Museum

Continue along Little Pier Street, up a ramp and follow the arrows to the *Powerhouse Museum*. The museum is the central showpiece of the Museum of Applied Arts and Science. It is Australia's largest museum, with over 25 exhibitions, and has occupied its present premises since 1988 when work was completed to convert the shell of the old *Ultimo Power Station*, (constructed 1899-1902) which provided power for Sydney's electric tram system. It's a great place to take the kids, with lots of hands on exhibits, and needs more than one visit to do it justice.

The museum dates back to the setting up of the 'Technological Industrial and Sanitary Museum' established with objects from the International Exhibition held in the Sydney Garden Palace in 1879. Its first curator, Joseph Maiden, a botanist, was later a director of the Botanical Gardens.

There is quite an extraordinary array of objects on display, relating to every branch of the applied sciences. Search out the Shorter-Slater collection of English Doulton porcelain; to say nothing of the displays of clothing, furniture, clocks, musical instruments, collections of weapons from swords through to machine guns and an exhibit tracing the development of calculations from Egyptian times to present day computers.

In a section on transport is the Bleriot monoplane, which in 1914 made the first flight from Sydney to Melbourne carrying 2000 souvenir postcards, Australia's first airmail. There's a life size replica of an Avro 504, used by the R.A.F. in World War I and the plane used by Qantas for its first commercial flight in 1920.

On its own train track inside the museum is Loco No.1, which pulled the first train in New South Wales

Sydney city and The Domain (previous pages). St.Marys Cathedral is at centre left and the Art Gallery of New South Wales at bottom right.

The gold crown of Sydney Tower (right), with Sydney's eastern suburbs and the Pacific Ocean in the background.

Saturday

信 厲 德 通

Dixon Street (above) in the centre of Sydney's Chinatown, is in the Haymarket, a suburb in the south of the city where Sydney's Chinese community settled after leaving The Rocks late in the nineteenth century.

A catalina flying boat in the Powerhouse Museum (top right).

Sydney Entertainment Centre (below right), Australia's largest indoor auditorium.

(and Australia) during trials on 24th May 1855. The locomotive was built at Robert Stephenson's works at Newcastle in 1854, and imported to Australia with three other identical locomotives for Sydney's first railway line which ran from Redfern to Parramatta. It retired from active service in 1877 and was acquired by the Museum in 1884. Behind the loco are some carriages, including an original 1854 third class carriage discovered in a field on a farm in the 1930s.

But the highlight of the museum's collection is an original Boulton and Watt steam engine, the third rotative (wheel turning) steam engine ever built and the oldest known steam engine in existence. The engine was installed in Whitbread's London brewery in 1785 to replace a mill wheel drawn by 24 horses used for grinding malt. In 1787 Samuel Whitbread entertained King George III and Queen Charlotte at his brewery, proudly showing off 'this Engine which performs the work of 35

Horfes'. The engine was a reliable source of power at Whitbreads for 102 years from 1785 to 1887, when it was replaced by a more powerful steam engine. One of the original trustees of the Museum of Applied Arts and Sciences, Professor Archibald Liversidge, happened to be in London at the time, heard about the change-over and persuaded Whitbreads to donate the engine to the museum. Quite recently a decision was made to restore the engine to steam driven power, and in

1985, on its 200th birthday, the engine was made to function again on steam power. Other exhibits may surprise you by suddenly springing to life in the Steam Revolution display, where steam powered electric generators, engines and fairground equipment are driven by the same source of steam power that drives the Boulton & Watt engine.

The Powerhouse is open 10.00am to 5.00pm daily (closed Christmas Day and Good Friday). There is a small entrance charge.

The Chinese Gardens

Make your way back towards the Pump House and walk under Pier Street to the southern end of Darling Harbour. Continue walking and after a short distance you can see on your right the *Chinese Gardens*. The "Garden of Friendship" was designed according to southern Chinese tradition by Sydney's sister city, Guangzhou in China. A double-storey pavilion, "the Gurr", stands above a surrounding system of interconnected lakes and waterfalls.

Intended to 'capture the mood of a forest refuge in the bustling city' the bubbling brooks and waterfalls backed by cherry and lychee trees are intended to represent the hills and mountain springs of a landscape in southern China. The garden is a place of mystery and secrets where you can let your imagination roam. Is that an irregular shaped rock jutting from the lotus pond; no, it's the head of a rock monster rising from the depths to guard its domain. And the twin pavilion of pear fragrance and lychee shadow – why does it only have six supporting posts when it should have eight?

Follow the pathways around the landscaped gardens and over bridges before resting at the Tea House where the scent of lotus flowers mingles with that of freshly brewed tea and traditional cakes. The Garden is open daily from 9.30am to 6.00pm. There is a small entrance charge.

Just north of the Gardens is *Sydney Sega World*, an indoor entertainment complex offering fun rides and virtual reality experiences, with just next door, the *IMAX Theatre* with the world's biggest movie screen.

The Exhibition Centre

Leaving the Gardens, walk through *Tumbalong Park* with its fountains and groves of native eucalypts. The Port Jackson Fig tree within the park is affectionately known as "Fred". On the left of the park lies the *Exhibition Centre* which covers a massive 25,000 square metres of column-free space under the one roof. Opened in January 1988, the centre is designed to hold major international exhibitions. The glassed eastern facade is stepped back in five separate stages that can be partitioned off to form smaller halls. The fifth hall is linked by a covered walkway to the Convention Centre. Continue north along walkways lined by palm trees and pass under the flyover to *Cockle Bay*.

On the left the seven storey Convention Centre provides seating for 3,500 people and houses modern

Aerial view of the Chinese Gardens (left page).

Details of some of the weird and wonderful fittings and architecture to stimulate the imagination in the Gardens (left).

communications, translation and audio-visual equipment that gives it the technology demanded on the international convention circuit. Inside the centre a restaurant and bar overlook the Waterfront Promenade and Cockle Bay.

Harbourside Festival Markets

Continue your stroll alongside Cockle Bay. On your left the *Harbourside Festival Market Place* has 200 shops to tease your wallet and 54 assorted food outlets to tempt your palate.

The National Maritime Museum

Walk underneath Pyrmont Bridge to the National Maritime Museum, which focuses on the history of Australia's links with the sea from the earliest times to the present. Alongside the museum's two wharves you can see a number of ships including the 'Vampire', a former RAN destroyer and 'Akarana', a restored 1888 11.9 metre gaff cutter

Saturday

which was New Zealand's Bicentennial gift to Australia. One of the most historically interesting vessels on display is the *Krait,* used on operation Jaywich during the Second World War. The *Krait* was a Singapore-based Japanese fishing boat captured in the early part of the war which carried a group of Australian commandos to Singapore Harbour to plant mines on Japanese shipping. Forty thousand tons of shipping went to the bottom of the Harbour and all the commandoes returned safely. Trace the evolution of the Aussie surfboard, and the development of the famous winged keel of Australia II. Australia II broke the longest winning run in sporting history in 1983 when she wrested the Americas Cup from the Americans at Newport Rhode Island. The yacht itself takes pride of place in the museum's central gallery with its soaring white wave-like roof. Nearby is Ken Warby's hydroplane, "Spirit of Australia", built in his back garden and powered by a Westinghouse jet engine

from a Neptune aircraft bought by Warby for $65. The boat still holds the world speed record on water of 511kmh set at Blowering Dam New South Wales in November 1977. A faster speed was actually set by Donald Campbell on 2nd January 1967 at Coniston Water in the U.K., but the record didn't stand because it wasn't over the measured distance. Campbell was killed in the attempt when his boat crashed.

If you're in the mood to lose your shirt, or win some money to buy a new one, *The Sydney Casino* is five minutes walk from the Museum.

Pyrmont Bridge

Exit the Maritime Museum, walk up the ramp onto *Pyrmont Bridge* and walk over the bridge in the direction of the city. A giant Australian flag flies from a flagpole mounted on a concrete pedestal in the water on the left. This is the Bicentennial flagpole, exactly 200 feet high, erected during the 1988 Bicentennial year. Halfway across the

bridge is the control cabin for the Pyrmont Bridge swing span, which regularly opens to allow leisure craft to pass into Cockle Bay. If the gate at the front of the control cabin is open, visitors are welcome to climb the steps and pay a visit. The central swing span of the bridge is one of the longest in the world and the first to use electric power, available in 1902 when Ultimo Power Station commenced generation. An ingenious device permits the Monorail beam, which runs above the bridge, to remain in place for the monorail to pass over if the swing bridge is opened for vessels up to 14 metres in height, or to swing open with the bridge for the passage of higher vessels. An automatic cut-out works in the latter case to prevent the monorail carriages plunging off the end of the rail into the harbour.

Sydney Aquarium

Descend the escalator at the east end of Pyrmont Bridge and turn left for *Sydney Aquarium* where 50 tanks and two walk-through oceanariums

have 350 species from Harbour prawns to saltwater crocodiles and the infamous Aussie shark. Don't miss the extraordinary display of Moray eels near the entrance inhabiting three piles of clay pipes. Open daily from 9.30am to 9.00pm.

Take the escalator back up to Pyrmont Bridge and walk up the steps to Darling Park Station to catch the monorail for an aerial view of Darling Harbour. Built by TNT Harbourlink in 1988, the Monorail runs in a 3.6 kilometre loop and has seven stations – Darling Park, Harbourside, Convention, Haymarket, World Square, Park Plaza (Town Hall) and City Centre. Buy a token at the station entrance. Children under four years old travel free.

St Andrew's Cathedral

Alight at Park Plaza (Town Hall). Outside the station, turn right into Pitt Street and then right again at Park Street and at George Street turn left and walk to *St.Andrews*

Cathedral. The foundation stone of the Cathedral was laid by Governor Macquarie on August 31, 1819, but construction was axed on the recommendation of Colonial Commissioner Bigge and the project wasn't restarted until 1837. Architect Edmund Blacket redesigned the Cathedral in "perpendicular Gothic" based on St.Mary's Church in Oxford England. The Cathedral was consecrated on St.Andrew's Day, November 30, 1868.

Edmund Thomas Blacket, (1817-1883), designer of the University, St.Andrew's and many other churches in Sydney, was buried originally in Balmain Cemetery. When the cemetery was turned into a park in 1941, the ashes of Blacket and his wife were re-interred under the floor in the south west corner of the Cathedral. On the north wall inside the Cathedral hangs a Union Jack which was carried by Mr. R. Fair of the Australian 8th Division while a P.O.W. in Singapore, on the Burma Railway, and to the coal mines of

Ohama in Japan, where it was flown on V.J. Day 1945 after taking down the Japanese flag.

A chapel in the north west corner of the cathedral is paved with marble salvaged from St.Pauls Cathedral London after it was bombed in the Second World War. Guided tours of the Cathedral depart daily at 11.00am and 1.45pm.

Continuing north on George Street, walk past the Italian Renaissance style *Sydney Town Hall,* opened in 1889. Before the Opera House was completed the Town Hall's Centennial Hall, with seating for 2,000 was Sydney's main concert venue. Famous organists go into raptures over the tonal excellence of the Centennial Hall's organ, one of the two largest original 19th century organs in the world, with 8,500 pipes.

The Queen Victoria Building

Cross Druitt Street to the *Queen Victoria Building,* a real cathedral of a shopping centre built in the 19th

Sydney Convention Centre (above).

The entry to Harbourside Festival Markets (below).

The control tower on Pyrmont Bridge (below) operates the swing mechanism of the bridge.

The Festival Markets at dusk (above), with the Novotel, Hotel Ibis and Mercure luxury apartments in the background.

Pyrmont Bridge (below). The white Sydney Aquarium and Hotel Nikko are on the east side of the bridge behind the Sydney Monorail train.

Saturday

century, occupying an entire city block between York and George Streets and containing 200 shops and restaurants. Sydney's, and some of the world's leading ladies' and mens' fashion houses are all collected together under one roof. Sit at one of the tables of the Old Vienna Coffee House on the landing at the north end of Albert Walk, listen to the classical piped music and wallow in the atmosphere of Victorian splendour.

Turn right on Market Street, and pass the *State Theatre*, at No.49, a lavishly decorated picture palace opened in 1929. Tours are subject to availability, and enquiries should be directed to Sydney Tower. The foyer of the theatre has a staircase of solid marble, and a mosaic floor depicting St George and the Dragon locked in mortal combat. In the theatre is the second biggest cut crystal chandelier in the world, and in the basement an engine from a First World War German submarine that used to power the stage lift. See the theatres' art gallery, and if you're lucky, the theatre ghost!

Sydney Tower

Cross Market Street and walk across the Pitt Street Mall to *Centrepoint*. Go up three flights of escalators to the Podium Level, where lifts leave for the Sydney Tower Observation deck, (there is a lift charge), or one floor down the Gallery Level is the access

points for lifts to the revolving restaurants (no lift charge).

Centrepoint is much more than just an observation tower. The ground floor and lower levels comprise a shopping centre with over 170 speciality shops, including many eateries on the Pitt Street level. The centre is linked by overhead walkways and underground promenades to the David Jones and Grace Bros Department Stores, flanking Centrepoint to the east and west. A 10 storey office building and a convention and exhibition centre sit on top of the Centrepoint retail levels.

The tower itself, rising 1,000 feet (304.8 metres) above street level, is slightly higher than the Eiffel Tower and the tallest building south of the equator. Its golden turret has a waiter service revolving restaurant, a cheaper informal self-select revolving restaurant, a function room and an observation level.

An exciting building in its design, many innovative techniques were employed in the construction of Sydney Tower. The stem is made from 46 barrel-shaped steel units stacked one on top of the other. The crowning golden turret and its white telecommunications antenna, together weighing nearly 2,000 tonnes, are locked onto the top of the stem, and anchored to the concrete roof of Centrepoint by 56 long

Aerial view of Darling Harbour and the city (above).

The National Maritime Museum (right). A ferry is heading for the wharf at the Sydney Aquarium at top left of the picture.

The destroyer 'Vampire' (right) at the National Maritime Museum, is the sister ship of the 'Voyager', sliced in two and sunk by the aircraft carrier 'Melbourne' in 1964 in Australia's worst peacetime naval disaster. The Vampire and Voyager were built for the Royal Australian Navy at Cockatoo Island in Sydney, to a British Naval design.

(Following pages) Left : Sydney got its own version of Versailles when the Town Hall was completed in 1889. The foundation stone was laid by Prince Alfred, Duke of Edinburgh, in 1868. Several different architects had a hand in the design.

The TNT Harbourlink Monorail wends its merry way through Sydney (right page).

133

Seven Days

Saturday

steel cables, made in Australia under a Swiss patent.

A 162,000 litre water tank, suspended on cables in the turret linked to mechanical dampers, oscillates at the same frequency as the tower but out of phase with it to minimise the sway of the tower in strong winds. It is amazing how effective this system is, for the tower stays as stiff as a ram-rod even in the most blustery conditions.

There couldn't be a better view of Sydney at lunchtime than from one of the restaurants in Sydney Tower, or for something more down to earth try one of the eateries on the third level of the *Skygarden*, 970 feet down off 166 Pitt Street.

If you've time to roam try the Picadilly Centre for size off Pitt Street. A quarry must have been kept busy for months producing the acres of amber marble. Not even banks can afford this sort of opulence these days, just the shopping centres they finance and can repossess.

Descending from the tower, from the Gallery Level of Centrepoint (green carpet) walk through the shops and over the enclosed pedestrian bridge spanning Castlereagh Street into *David Jones*. Go down the escalator to the ground floor, and be prepared to mislay your credit cards, because the entire ground floor, in a most elegant grey marble setting, is devoted to the sale of everything for

the well-dressed lady, with belts, stockings, handbags, jewellery, perfumes and cosmetics in abundance.

Turn right outside the Elizabeth Street entrance to David Jones and cross Market Street to the *Sheraton on the Park Hotel* at 161 Elizabeth Street. The hotel has a dramatic entrance foyer flanked by giant burgundy coloured marble columns. Enjoy a refreshing drink seated near the fountain in the tea lounge on the first floor conservatory looking across to *Hyde Park*.

On the same side of Elizabeth Street a little further along is the *Sydney Synagogue* and museum, open to the public 12noon to 1.00pm on Tuesdays and 1.00pm to 2.00 pm on

Sydney city centre (left) with the Aquarium and Hotel Nikko at bottom right. If you have a sharp eye you may just be able to pick out the Queen Victoria Building in the opening between two buildings.

St.Andrews Cathedral (below), with a foundation stone laid by Governor Macquarie on 31st August, 1819, is the oldest cathedral in Australia. However, construction was abandoned on the recommendation of Colonial Commissioner Bigger, and the present structure was built between 1837-68.

east through the park and pass the *Archibald Fountain*, a collection of statues from Greek Mythology spouting water and cross College Street to St Mary's Cathedral. A cannon facing College Street at the north east corner of Hyde Park, cast at the Carron Works, Scotland in 1806, once formed part of the armament of Fort Macquarie, which stood on Bennelong Point before Sydney Opera House.

The site of St Mary's was granted by Governor Macquarie to the first official chaplain to the colony of N.S.W., Father Joseph Therry who arrived in 1820. Macquarie laid the foundation stone of the Cathedral the following year. The original St Mary's burnt down on June 29 1865 and all that remains is part of a pillar east of the present church near the entrance to the crypt. At the Coroner's inquest into the fire, Constable Cannon, who was on duty close to the Cathedral at ten past nine on the evening of 29th of June, recalled

Thursdays. Pedestrian access to the Great Synagogue is from the west side of the building around the block in Castlereagh Street.

Cross Elizabeth Street to Hyde Park, set aside by Governor Phillip as a common 'never to be granted or let lease on'. In 1810 Macquarie deemed 'The whole of the open ground yet unoccupied in the vicinity of the town of Sydney, hitherto known and alternately called by the names of "The Common", "Exercising Ground", "Cricket Ground", and "Race Course"… being intended in future for the recreation and amusement of the inhabitants of the Town, and as a field of exercise for the troops.

The Governor has thought proper to name the ground "Hyde Park" by which name it is henceforth to be called…' Macquarie's Highlanders cleared the bush and laid out Sydney's first racecourse, two kilometres long. The first horse race held in Sydney at the course in October 1810 was won by William Wentworth (of Vaucluse House), son of D'Arcy Wentworth (of Sydney Hospital). William won the race on one of his father's horses, which were stabled at D'Arcy's estate called Homebush in the west of Sydney, the site chosen for Sydney's 2000 Olympics. The park was also the site of Sydney's first cricket pitch. Take the path running north

'… I happened to look towards the southern gable of the Cathedral, and I then saw a light glimmering in the three top windows; thinking they might have forgotten to put the lights out (the constable walked to the Cathedral and)… looking through the aperture in the middle of the doors, I saw that the high alter was all in flames… not being able to get into the Cathedral (he raised the alarm and) returned and saw the fire breaking out through the window at the back of the high alter, and coming out through the roof; it was a great solid flame of fire, and I think it must have been burning some time before I saw it.'

Saturday

The Queen Victoria Building (right and below) designed by Sydney City Council Architect George McRae in Romanesque style to resemble a Byzantine Palace as a 'municipal market on the scale of a cathedral', was constructed between 1893 and 1898. The market was not a commercial success, and in the 1930s the interior galleries were concreted over and partitioned for council offices, and the Sydney City Library. After talk of pulling the 'monstrosity' down, it was decided the Queen Victoria Building should be preserved. The Malaysian company Ipoh Garden Berhad carried out a mammoth restoration project between January 1984 and November 1986 at a cost of 80 million dollars, in return for a 99 year lease on the site.

Right page : the magnificent foyer of the State Theatre on Market Street.

Saturday

Centrepoint Tower from Hyde Park (right).

Right Page :

The grand entry of the Sheraton on the Park (top left).

The rose window of Sydney Synagogue (top right). The Synagogue was designed by Thomas Rowe, architect of Sydney Hospital.

The traffic lights turn blue tomorrow, or in this case orange. At least the sky is always blue in Sydney. St.Marys Cathedral from Prince Albert Road (centre). Pope Paul VI, the first Pope to visit Australia, celebrated mass in the Cathedral on 30th November,1970.

The Sandringham Garden (bottom), in Hyde Park close to the corner of College and Park Streets, is a memorial to Kings George V and VI. It was opened on 5th February 1954 by Queen Elizabeth and the Duke of Edinburgh.

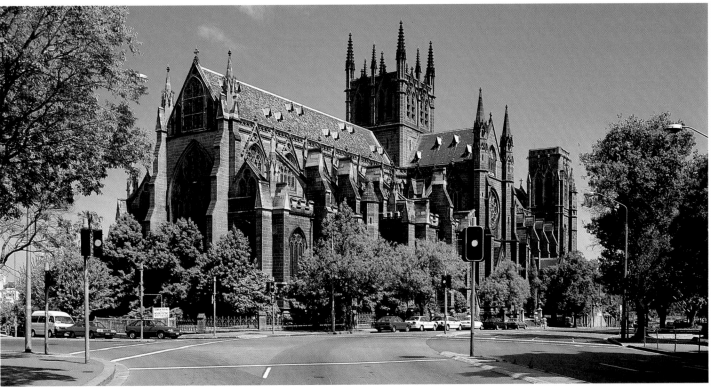

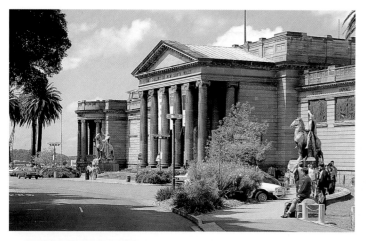

The Art Gallery of New South Wales (top left).

The statue of Burns on Art Gallery Road in the Domain (top right). The statue stands in a garden named after him – a traditional gathering place for Scots in Sydney.

The Archibald Fountain (above), erected in 1932 was bequeathed to the people of Australia by J. F. Archibald, publisher of The Bulletin magazine, to commemorate the association of Australia and France in the 1914-18 war. The figures from Greek Mythology are by Parisian Sculptor François Sicard.

Detail of the stonework on St.Marys Cathedral (above right).

U.S. sailors and local girls outside the Art Gallery (top right) when the American fleet was in town. The reclining figure in the background is Angles 1980, by Henry Moore.

New designs were drawn up by architect William Wardell, construction was started in 1868, the Cathedral was in use by 1882 and was finished September 2, 1928. Two spires topping the south facing towers that were part of the design, were never completed, and the bishop has promised that the first benefactor who comes up with the necessary funds to build them can have their name on them.

A copy of Michaelangelo's La Pieta, sculpted from white marble in Carrara Italy by Nicoli Sicmas at the "Laboratorie Artistico" is just inside the west entrance facing Hyde Park. Visitors are welcome to walk around the Cathedral except when services are on. Guided tours of the Cathedral take place at twelve o-clock every Sunday, or a self guide booklet about the Cathedral can be picked up inside. The inlay of the floor of the crypt (open office hours only) and the mosaic floor of the sanctuary are worth seeing. The stained glass windows of the cathedral were made by Hardman Bros. in England. A scene of Macquarie laying the first foundation stone of the church is depicted in the lower panel of one of the stained glass windows above the aisle of the west nave. The bells of St.Mary's, cast in the foundry of Whitechapel London in 1985 and installed June 1986 are the sister peal to Canterbury Cathedral in England.

The Art Gallery

From St.Mary's walk north on College Street into Prince Albert Road past the Tudor style Registrar General Department building (modelled on Hampton Court London) and enter *The Domain* at Art Gallery Road. Next to the road are a pair of stone gateposts. In 1817 after Macquarie enclosed the Domain with walls and paling fences he decreed that entry would only be permitted during daylight hours. The lodge next to the gateposts was built in 1835 as the gatekeepers residence. In 1860 the Minister for Lands, John Robertson ruled the

gates should be left open at all times and the Domain has been accessible to the public for 24 hours a day ever since. The people of Sydney erected a statue of Robertson in the Domain in gratitude, which stands west of the Art Gallery.

Continue on Art Gallery Road past the statue of Burns to the Art Gallery of New South Wales; open daily from 10.00am to 5.00pm. The building housed the National Art Gallery until it moved to Canberra. Entry to the Art Gallery is free, although if a travelling world exhibition is on display there may be a charge for that section. The Gallery has permanent exhibitions on 18th to 20th century Australian Art, 17th to 20th century European Art, neoclassical sculptures and Asian Art. Among the 19th century European paintings don't miss 'The defence of Rorke's Drift 1880' by French painter, Alphonse de Neuville.

A new wing of the Gallery opened in December 1988. Its four levels include a sculpture garden, contemporary collections of Australian and European prints and drawings, 20th century British and European art, an impressionist exhibition as well as a new coffee shop and theatre space.

Fort Denison

If there's still time, you may wish to round off the day with a visit to *Fort Denison,* organised through Captain Cook Cruises on Wharf Six at Circular Quay.

Alternatively, if you've had enough of colonial relics, a *Captain Cook Cruise* can be booked instead.

When the First Fleet arrived in Sydney, "Rock Island", as it was then known, was a convenient place to punish recalcitrant convicts, who were left in chains on the island for a week on bread and water. In November 1796 an Irish convict, Francis Morgan, who had been found guilty of a particularly brutal murder, was rowed out to the island and hanged and his body left to rot on the gallows as a deterrent to others. Before he was despatched, folk-lore has it that upon being asked if he had anything further to say, Morgan calmly surveyed the scenery from the top of Rock Island and said, 'Well it certainly is a fine harbour you have here'.

One night in December 1839 two American warships that sailed into the harbour were only noticed when their presence was revealed at first light the following morning. To improve harbour defences, Governor Gipps ordered that a fort be built on Rock Island. The island was quarried to the waterline but the necessary funds were not forthcoming from the British Government and it wasn't until 1855, and the onset of the Crimean War, that construction of the fort finally went ahead. Colonel George Barney, who built Victoria Barracks and Circular Quay, designed the fort. The martello tower was designed by Government Architect Edmund Blacket. When it was opened in 1857 the fort was named after the Governor of N.S.W., Sir William Denison.

The guided tour of Fort Denison (top).

Fort Denison (below). The magazine where explosives were stored and the gun room with its three canons in the martello tower, look just the same today as when the Fort was completed in 1858. The Fort is the central tide register for New South Wales and the caretaker is responsible for taking readings from the measuring equipment in a room next to the martello tower. During the Second World War two anti-aircraft guns were mounted on the Fort, one on top of the martello tower and one on the west battlement, (bottom left of picture).

The guns of the fort were never fired in anger, although the fort once came under fire, albeit accidentally. During the Japanese midget submarine attack on Sydney in 1942, a shell from the American cruiser U.S.S. Chicago, fired at one of the submarines, hit Fort Denison's martello tower leaving a crack that can still be seen in the top of the tower wall.

Tonight, return to George Street and descend the stairs between the escalators at the entrance to the

Hilton Hotel opposite the central dome of the Queen Victoria Building, to the Marble Bar in the basement. The bar was originally part of the 1890 Adams Hotel, owned by George Adams, a farm labourer from Hertfordshire who made a fortune holding public sweepstakes on horse races in the 1880s. Determined to make the bar of his hotel the most opulent in Sydney and with money no object, Adams spent the then astronomical sum of £32,000 decorating his bar in

15th century Italian renaissance style. Fireplaces and columns were solid marble and the walls were hung with a series of 18 paintings by the Australian artist Julian Ashton featuring countryside scenes replete with voluptuous nudes. The twin bars of American walnut were sculptured with figures that amply complemented the paintings.

When the George Adams Hotel was demolished in 1968 the bar was classified by the National Trust as a First-Class Monument. The bar and all the marble fittings of the interior were painstakingly dismantled and numbered then re-erected in the basement of the Hilton Hotel ready for its opening in 1973.

The fact that fourteen of the original eighteen Julian Ashton nudes still decorate the Marble Bar's walls, perchance contributed to the bar once winning Australian Playboy's survey for Best Bar in Australia.

Circular Quay and the city (above).

SUNDAY

Sunday

Exclusive suburbs and magnificent beaches

Leaving Circular Quay then walking through the Royal Botanic Gardens, to-day's route includes a stop at Elizabeth Bay House, a journey by cab around the exclusive harbourside eastern suburbs of Darling Point and Point Piper, a trip by flying boat from Rose Bay to Palm Beach, then a return journey back to Sydney through the northern beaches, and via the scenic Wakehurst Parkway and Eastern Valley Way.

Walk south on Phillip Street at the eastern end of Circular Quay, then turn left up Albert Street. Turn right on Macquarie Street and pass the east facade of the Treasury, then turn left and following the road to the rear of the N.S.W. Conservatorium of Music, enter through the gate into the Royal Botanic Gardens.

The site of the gardens was the first place in Sydney to be successfully cultivated by members of the First Fleet. By July 1788 on some alluvial soil either side of a small stream that ran into Farm Cove, a Government Farm had been established with 'nine acres of corn'. One of the Tolpuddle Martyrs, Joseph Gerrald, transported in 1794, built a cottage and farmed the area. Gerrald died in 1796 and was buried east of the creek.

Mrs Macquarie's Road

In 1816 Governor Macquarie completed a road about three kilometres long that ran from Old Government House around Farm Cove to the Point and back to Government House. Macquarie's wife, Elizabeth, made daily journeys in her carriage on the road and would stop at the point to relax and admire the scenery. That same year Macquarie appointed Charles Fraser, a soldier from his 46th Regiment of Highlanders to the post of 'Superintendent of the Botanic Gardens'.

Fraser visited Norfolk Island and New Zealand, Tasmania, Western Australia and Queensland collecting plants and seeds and exchanged seeds with other botanists overseas. Fraser died in 1831. His successor, Richard Cunningham was speared to death by aborigines on the Bogan River collecting plant specimens whilst on Thomas Mitchell's expedition of 1835. Ever since, an appointment as live-in Superintendent of the Botanic Gardens has been accepted with pride and as an honour, with most Superintendents holding the post for 20 or more years. Charles Moore enjoyed a particularly long stint as Superintendent for 48 years from 1848-1896.

The Gardens were renamed the *Royal Botanic Gardens* following the visit of Queen Elizabeth in 1954, the first reigning British Monarch to visit the country. She stepped ashore in Sydney at the Botanic Gardens on the east side of Farm Cove.

Amble through the gardens at will, to arrive at *Mrs Macquarie's Point*. Whichever direction you take the Gardens are delightful. The Australian native plants have the blue labels. Lookout for some of the 95 species of birds that have been seen in the Gardens over the years, you have a good chance of spotting

Barrenjoey Lighthouse on Palm Beach (previous pages).

Sulphur crested cockatoos (right) that frequent the Botanic Gardens, are quite a menace, uprooting plants and causing expensive damage to nearby roof-tops.

Sydney Opera House (below), from The Domain, near Mrs Macquarie's Chair.

149

'I have just returned from the most beautiful spot I ever saw – the Botanical Gardens of Sydney. It was literally a walk through Paradise… The intensity of one's admiration is almost painful', wrote John Hood in 1843 and the same superlatives apply today.

A statue of Venus (right).

Aerial view of the lake (centre).

The tree with branches like the coils of a snake haired hydra (far right) is a swamp white oak, a native of south eastern Canada and eastern U.S.A.

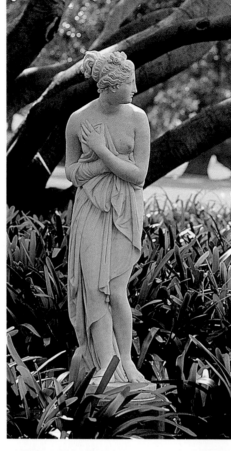

The sandstone monument (right) is a replica of the Choragic Monument of Lysicrates, erected in Athens about 330 B.C.

Sunday

Mrs Macquarie's Chair (above). Elizabeth Campbell, wife of the Governor, used to ride from Government House in her carriage and stop at the stone bench to sit and gaze at the view of the harbour.

A section of the azalea garden (right).

the common ones, Kookaburras, Sulphur-crested Cockatoos, White Ibis and the Blue Wren. At dusk Brush-tailed Possums come out and at certain times of the year Flying Foxes descend on the Gardens in great numbers.

Next to the creek just south of the kiosk, in the centre of the gardens, a small plaque marks the site of the first Government Farm. On the east side of Farm Cove near the Fleet Stairs, a plain sandstone wall decorated with the Royal Crest com-memorates the landing of Queen Elizabeth in 1954.

At the bus stop on Mrs Macquarie's Road near the Point, the regular *Sydney Explorer Bus* can be picked up which will take you to *Elizabeth Bay House*. Alternatively, it's about half an hour's walk. If you opt for the latter, follow the path around the point, past *Mrs Macquarie's Chair*, a seat cut in the rock where Elizabeth Henriette Campbell used to wile away many hours enjoying the scenery. Some rock alcoves in the sandstone next to the path were used as shelters by unemployed, homeless men during the depression. After five minutes walk you will pass *The Andrew (Boy) Charlton Pool* on Woolloomooloo Bay. In 1924, 16 year old Andrew Charlton beat Arne Borg the Swedish World Champion in a race at the Domain Baths, just here. Charlton went on to win a gold and silver medal at the Paris Olympics.

A few minutes walk after passing the pool, descend a flight of concrete

The Palm Grove (left) was established in 1853 and contains over 140 different kinds of palms. Many of the palms collected during the nineteenth century were grown with the possibility in mind they may one day be farmed commercially for oil, palm sugar or fibre industries in Australia.

Grove of eucalypts in The Domain (left).

Sunday

steps past an electric sub-station into Lincoln Crescent, turn left along Cowper Wharf Roadway passing the Bells Hotel and Woolloomooloo Bay Hotel, then as you turn into Brougham Street ascend the broad flight of *McElhone Stairs* directly in front.

Garden Island

Walking through the gardens on *Woolloomooloo Bay* and as you climb McElhone Stairs you will, no doubt, have noticed some destroyers and other ships moored at *Garden Island Naval Base*. As its name implies, the base was once an 11 acre island lying 200 metres off Potts Point. When the First Fleet landed the

sailors from *HMS Sirius* cleared the vegetation on part of the island for a vegetable garden, hence the name. On some rocks on top of the island the initials of some of the sailors have been carved with the date 1788. The calling cards of these First Fleet Kilroys are protected by three glass pyramids.

In 1857 the island was granted by the N.S.W. Government to the Royal Navy for use as a base. A number of buildings dating from around this time including residences, a barracks, a factory, stores and administration buildings still exist. In 1904 Garden Island was handed over to the Australian Commonwealth. It has been Australia's biggest naval

base ever since, playing an important role as a re-supply depot for allied shipping through two World Wars.

On May 31, 1942, three Japanese midget submarines entered Sydney Harbour. A torpedo fired at ships moored at Garden Island, hit the wharf next to the Kuttabul, an old ferry being used as a dormitory, blowing off the stern of the ferry and killing 19 ratings. Two of the submarines were sunk by depth charges, the third was never found. The two damaged submarines were recovered and their best halves were welded together to make a complete submarine, which takes pride of place outside the Australian War Museum in Canberra.

Aerial view of the Royal Botanic Gardens and city (far left).

Garden Island Naval Base and Woolloomooloo Bay (left).

Between 1940 and 1944 the island was joined to the mainland by the reclamation of 14 hectares of seabed during the building of the *Captain Cook Dry Dock,* a considerable feat of engineering at the time. Garden Island is open on special occasions, advertised in the local press.

Elizabeth Bay House

At the top of McElhone Stairs cross leafy Victoria Street walk to the end of Challis Avenue, cross Macleay Street, walk through the alley opposite and turn right on Onslow Avenue to reach *Elizabeth Bay House.*

Elizabeth Bay House, in a quiet cul-de-sac on Elizabeth Bay, with a view overlooking the harbour, is a world away from the sleaze of Kings Cross just around the corner. The unpretentious exterior gives no clue to the treasure-trove of antiques within. The domed saloon of Elizabeth Bay House and elliptical stairway are considered particularly excellent examples of colonial architecture.

In October 1826, *Alexander John Macleay,* who had recently arrived from England to take up a post as Colonial Secretary, was granted 54 acres of land at Elizabeth Bay. Macleay employed the architect John Verge to design a 'Grecian Villa' for the site. Built between 1835 and 1838 the completed house was regarded as the finest in the colony.

When the house passed out of the ownership of the Macleay Family early this century, the rot quickly set in. A Botanical Garden surrounding the house was engulfed by development, the kitchen wing was demolished and the house was successively a colony for artists, a venue for society weddings and dances, partitioned and turned into 15 flats and finally an unused residence for the Lord Mayor of Sydney. The rot stopped in 1977, when the Historic Houses Trust of N.S.W. acquired Elizabeth Bay House and painstakingly restored it to the period of 1838-1845.

Elizabeth Bay (above). Elizabeth Bay House is at the centre right of the picture.

Elizabeth Bay House (right) built between 1835-38 for Colonial Secretary Alexander Macleay, was considered the finest house in the colony. Designed as a 'Grecian Villa' with a surrounding verandah, the house was never completed to architect John Verge's drawings because the cost of the house bankrupted Macleay.

In 1845 when Alexander Macleay was in financial trouble, he sold the house to his son and the contents were sold to furnish the newly completed Government House. An inventory made of the contents at the time still exists, so it has been possible to faithfully reproduce the furnishings of the period. In 1873 William John Macleay, Alexander Macleay's son's cousin, donated the family's insect, botanical, anthropological and geological collections to Sydney University where they can be viewed today in the Macleay Museum.

Rushcutters Bay

Hail a cab and head east on Bayswater and New South Head Roads. After descending the hill from Kings Cross, pass on the left a wide expanse of park fronting onto *Rushcutters Bay*, where hundreds of yachts are berthed at several marinas.

Rushcutters Bay Park is on reclaimed marshland that once extended inland from the bay. In May 1788 two convicts who were sent to cut rushes for thatch at the

St Mark's Church Darling Point (left).

*Terraced houses on Roslyn Gardens (left)
not far from Elizabeth Bay House.*

Sunday

Previous pages : Sydney Harbour. Rose Bay and Point Piper are in the foreground. Charles Von Hugel, who arrived in Sydney after Piper had 'been obliged to retire to the interior' wrote in 1833 that 'In Sydney Captain Piper's parties are talked of as of a glorious vanished age'.

Whale Beach and Palm Beach (right) with Pittwater and Broken Bay in the background.

Palm Beach (above).

Pittwater (below right). Scotland Island is at the centre of the picture.

bay, were killed by aborigines and had their tools stolen.

Darling Point

Turn left on Darling Point Road. Pass *St Marks Church* on the right, where Elton John was married and the *'Swifts'* on the left, a crenellated mansion similar to Government House built last century for the owner of a brewery and until recently the official residence of the Catholic Archbishop of Sydney. At the end of Darling Point Road, the recently opened *McKell Park* enjoys good views of the Harbour and nearby *Clark Island*.

Backtrack on Darling Point Road and turn left at St Mark's Church into Greenoaks Avenue, pass *'Bishopscourt'* on the right, residence of the Anglican Archbishop of Sydney, turn left at Ocean Avenue,

right at William Street past *Double Bay* and then left at the end of William Street to rejoin New South Head Road. After a short distance turn left on Wolseley Road and make a quick circuit of *Point Piper* on Wyuna and Wunulla Roads; who knows where they get the names from, but these unlikely addresses include some of the most valuable harbourside homes in Sydney.

Rose Bay

Rejoining New South Head Road pay off the cab at *Lyne Park* on *Rose Bay*. The Police Station at Rose Bay Park on the corner of Wunulla Road and New South Head Road was once the lodge for Woollahra House (1871), pulled down by developers before the war.

Rose Bay has been associated with flying contraptions since the

very earliest days of manned flight. *Lawrence Hargrave* the pioneer plane designer whose portrait appeared on the back of the old Australian $20 note, had a house at Point Piper overlooking Rose Bay and would fly kites over the Bay testing his designs. Later Rose Bay became Sydney's International Airport. Before the war 'Empire' flying boats of Imperial Airways and Qantas Airways offered services to the U.K. and across the Tasman to New Zealand.

It is thought that the flying boat base was the target of a Japanese submarine that surfaced off Bondi Beach and shelled Rose Bay on the night of June 7, 1942. Regular flying boat services continued to operate from Rose Bay to Norfolk and Lord Howe Islands until 1974.

Sunday

*Avalon Beach (top left) was named by
Arthur Small in the 1920s after the
mythical Avalon from the Irish fable.
Small sold blocks of land in the area.*

Bilgola Beach (centre left). Government surveyor James Meehan called the beach 'Belgoula' in 1814 after an aboriginal word meaning 'swirling waters'.

Newport and Newport Beach (left).

Whale Beach (above) with Pittwater and Ku-ring-gai Chase National Park in the background.

Sunday

Bungan Beach (above) is quiet even on the hottest summer days because the only access is by two long steep tracks.

A trip by flying boat

From the wharf at *Lyne Park* South Pacific Seaplanes fly four seater seaplanes on charter flights to Cronulla, the Hawkesbury district, Gosford and Palm Beach. There are marvellous views of Sydney's northern beaches and Pittwater on a flight to Palm Beach. To go on a flight, arrangements must be made in advance by calling South Pacific Seaplanes direct.

First Class Restaurants

If you want to do things in real style, charter a South Pacific Seaplane flight to take you to one of the restaurants on the Hawkesbury Estuary in the vicinity of Palm Beach. The restaurants front onto the water and the plane will taxi to the pontoon at the restaurant so you can alight directly at your destination. There are a few to choose from, including the Pasadena, Peat's Bite and what's generally regarded as one of the best restaurants in Australia, The Berowra Waters Inn. Alternatively there is Jonahs, overlooking Whale Beach, a short free ride in a taxi by road from Palm Beach.

Separate arrangements must be made for the restaurant and the flight. Prices for the restaurants reflect the standard of food and service and with all the trimmings and wine, expect to pay $60 to $100 per head.

Palm Beach

Near the shops on the Pittwater side of *Palm Beach*, ferries cross to secluded beaches on the west side of Pittwater and cruise boats depart to ply the Hawkesbury River system.

A brisk half-hour walk from the flying boat jetty north on Barrenjoey Beach to a walking track, following the route of an old horse drawn railway, takes you up to the lighthouse on the top of *Barrenjoey Head*. From the Head there are fantastic views looking south to the peninsula of Palm Beach, and north to Broken Bay, the entrance to the Hawkesbury River system.

Colonial Architect James Barnet designed the 11 metre high lighthouse, completed in 1881. The first lighthouse keeper, George Mulhall, died after being struck by lightning while he was collecting firewood during a storm. By rummaging around in the bush on the ocean side of the head, east of the lighthouse, you will find his grave. The memorial on his grave, erected by his son, reads –

'All ye that come my grave to see
Prepare in time to follow me
Repent at once without delay
For I in haste was called away'.

The Northern Beaches

Back at Palm Beach you can take the seaplane to return to Rose Bay,

Bongin Bongin Bay and Mona Vale Beach.

165

The Wakehurst Parkway, opened March 1946 (left) named after Lord Wakehurst, Governor of New South Wales 1937-46, runs through 25 square kilometres of undeveloped bushland.

Rearing above the road like the boundary of some medieval kingdom, Northbridge (right) was built as a private venture in 1889 by the North Sydney Tramway and Development Company to help sell real estate on the far side of Salt Pan Cove. The original suspension bridge was condemned in 1936, and the present reinforced concrete bridge retaining the original battlemented towers, was opened in 1939.

take the 190 bus that runs the 39 kilometres to Wynyard Station in the city, or take a cab back to the city along a more meandering route than the bus, to see the rest of the northern beaches that we missed on Thursday.

If you decide to take up the last option, start at *Governor Phillip Park* on Barrenjoey Road, stay on Ocean Road as it follows Palm Beach, turn right onto Palm Beach Road, then left into Florida Road. Florida Road winds past *Wiltshire and Hordern Parks*, filled with palm groves overlooking the southern end of Palm Beach then joins Whale Beach Road, with glimpses through the trees on your left of the ocean and Palm Beach. As Whale Beach Road rounds *Little Head* there's a good view of *Whale Beach* down below.

Stay on Whale Beach Road, turn left on Barrenjoey Road at the 'T' junction and follow Barrenjoey Road for one or two kilometres to *Avalon Beach*. It's not possible to see Avalon Beach from the road, turn

left at the traffic lights near the petrol station into Surfside Avenue to look down onto the relatively unspoilt stretch of Avalon Beach.

Rejoining Barrenjoey Road, turn left after a kilometre into The Serpentine, which, just like a serpent, winds round and down through a palm grove past *Bilgola Beach* and up and round again to rejoin Barrenjoey Road.

Stay on Barrenjoey Road past *Newport Beach* and take Hillcrest Avenue, the eighth turn on the left, leading to *Mona Vale Headland Reserve*. From the reserve there are great views right along *Mona Vale Beach* on one side and to quiet *Bungan Beach* on the other.

The Wakehurst Parkway

Backtrack to Barrenjoey Road, which soon runs into Pittwater Road at *Mona Vale*. Stay on Pittwater Road through several sets of traffic lights then fork right at *Narrabeen Lakes* onto the Wakehurst Parkway, following a signpost for Sydney. The

Wakehurst Parkway follows a picturesque route along the shore of *Narrabeen Lagoon* then through unspoilt bushland to a main intersection at *Warringah Road*.

Turn right at Warringah Road through the suburbs of Frenchs Forest and Forestville, cross Middle Harbour over the *Roseville Bridge*, then at the second set of traffic lights after crossing the bridge, fork left onto *Eastern Valley Way*. Following Eastern Valley Way for some kilometres as it gently winds and undulates through the suburbs of Castle Cove and Castlecrag, cross the castellated Cammeray Bridge at Northbridge and at the second set of traffic lights after the bridge, turn left onto the main Expressway over the Harbour Bridge and back to the city.

Tonight, to cap off an exciting week, why not treat yourself to an evening meal at the *Bennelong Restaurant* at the Opera House. The food is good and the setting unique.

Sunday

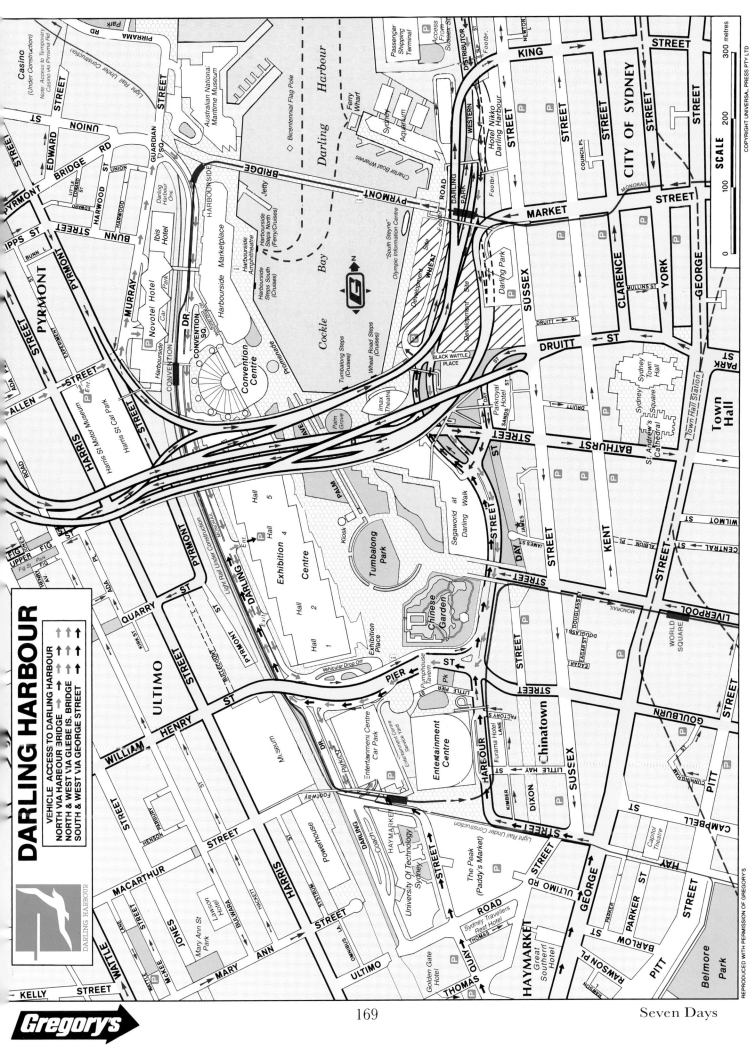

DARLING HARBOUR

VEHICLE ACCESS TO DARLING HARBOUR
NORTH VIA HARBOUR BRIDGE
NORTH & WEST VIA GLEBE IS. BRIDGE
SOUTH & WEST VIA GEORGE STREET

DARLING HARBOUR

Gregory's

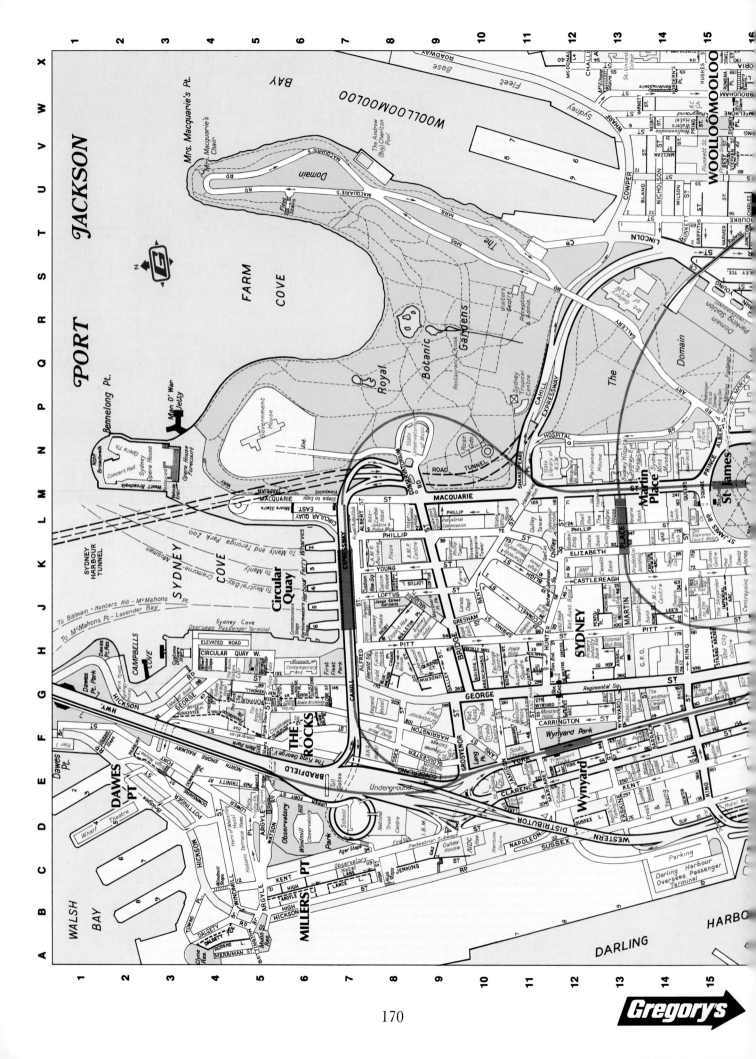

Gregory's

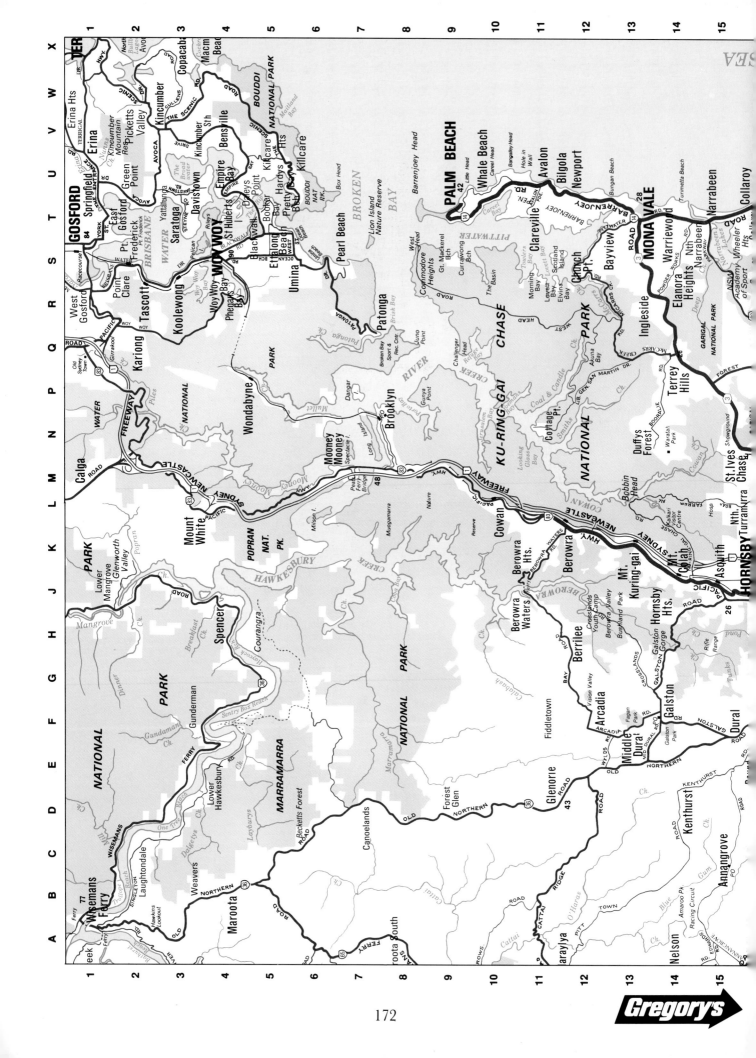

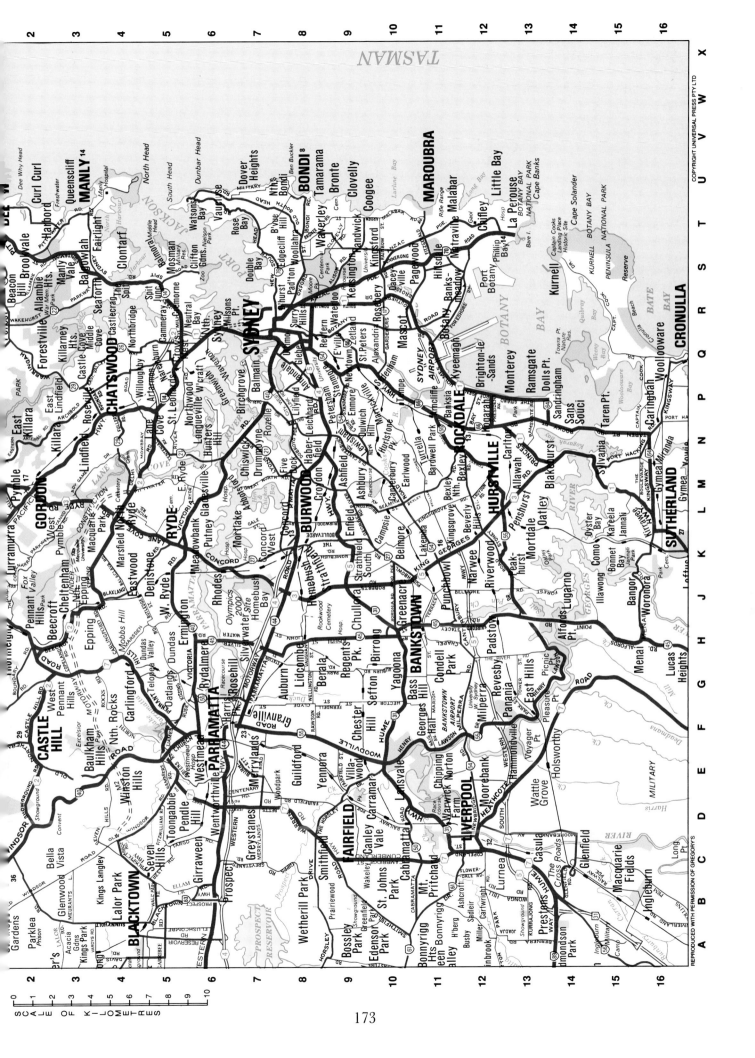

Index

Acknowledgements

Many of the photos in this book are aerials, which wouldn't have been possible without the pilots of Heli-Aust, Sydney Helicopter Service and, in particular, John Barnao of Helicopter Charter who could always be relied upon to position the helicopter in just the right place to get the shot that was required.

While on the subject of transport, I couldn't have got to all the places on the ground without my trusty 24-year-old Holden HD. It has been round the clock at least once but has just kept on keeping on. Thank you Holden for making such a reliable car. Though since publication of the first edition I now possess a 1983 Holden Commodore, which has also been round the clock twice and keeps on keeping on.

All the pictures except for a handful were taken on Pentax 35 mm and Pentax 6 x 7 photographic equipment. The cameras literally never let me down. Not once. Thank you Pentax for making such reliable cameras. However thanks don't go to the thief who broke into my house in May 1987 while I was dropping the kids off at school one morning, and relieved me of every camera and lens. May you rot in hell. And still rot in hell.

The film used for all the updated shots in this edition was Fuji Velvia 50 ASA slide film. There's no better slide film on the market for this sort of work.

Great appreciation must be extended to all the people who gave me access to rooftops and balconies to take photos from. I won't name you, but you know who you are, many thanks. Thanks also to the staff at the Mitchell and State Libraries for their cooperation in making material available for copying.

On the production side Ian Richards turned my original 'rough' into a workable design, made useful suggestions in designing the type and pasted up the initial photo-stat. Thank you Uncle Graham, for doing the proofreading. Max Peatman made the finishing touches to the layout, assembled the positional prints and final type, and offered many constructive comments about books and the book trade as we slogged away to get the artwork finished and sent to the plate-makers.

Dean Gardiner of Universal Press Pty Ltd, arranged permission for us to reproduce the maps and Face photo-headliners set the type on the cover. Well – they set the original type, which remains unchanged, but Face have since done an about-face and gone out of business.

Finally, thanks are extended to God, or whoever it was that created the natural wonder of Sydney Harbour, and to the planners, builders, engineers and architects, past and present, who built Sydney, 'Cos if it wasn't there, I couldn't have photographed it.